100

THE ROUGH GUIDE TO THE
BEST PLACES
ON EARTH 2022

100

THE ROUGH GUIDE TO THE
BEST PLACES
ON EARTH 2022

DISTRIBUTION

UK, Ireland and Europe
Apa Publications (UK) Ltd; sales@roughguides.com

United States and Canada
Ingram Publisher Services; ips@ingramcontent.com

Australia and New Zealand
Booktopia; retailer@booktopia.com.au

Worldwide
Apa Publications (UK) Ltd; sales@roughguides.com

SPECIAL SALES, CONTENT LICENSING AND CO-PUBLISHING

Rough Guides can be purchased in bulk quantities at discounted prices. We can create special editions, personalized jackets and corporate imprints tailored to your needs. Email: sales@roughguides.com
roughguides.com

Printed in Poland

A catalogue record for this book is available from the British Library

The publishers and authors have done their best to ensure the accuracy and currency of all the information in The Rough Guide to the 100 Best Places on Earth 2022, however, they can accept no responsibility for any loss, injury, or inconvenience sustained by any traveller as a result of information or advice contained in the guide.

HELP US UPDATE

We've gone to a lot of effort to ensure that this first edition of The Rough Guide to the 100 Best Places on Earth 2022 is accurate and up-to-date. But if you feel we've got it wrong or left something out, we'd like to know.

Please send your comments with the subject line "Rough Guide 100 Best Places Update" to mail@uk.roughguides.com. We'll credit all contributions and send a copy of the next edition (or any other Rough Guide if you prefer) for the very best emails.

THE ROUGH GUIDE TO THE
100 BEST PLACES ON EARTH
2022

Senior editor: Helen Fanthorpe

Picture editors: Aude Vauconsant & Tom Smyth

Designer: Michal Ptasznik

Head of DTP and pre-press: Rebeka Davies

B2B coordinator and typesetter: Daniel May

Proofreader: Samantha Cook

Head of Publishing: Sarah Clark

100

THE ROUGH GUIDE TO THE BEST PLACES ON EARTH 2022

USA, MEXICO & CANADA

CENTRAL AMERICA, SOUTH AMERICA & THE CARIBBEAN

OCEANIA

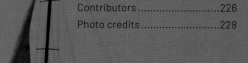

INTRODUCTION

From the raw mountainscapes of the Canadian Rockies to the time-warped charms of Fez medina, the modernist homes of Palm Springs and the tangled rainforests of Borneo, let Rough Guides take you on a journey to the 100 Best Places on Earth 2022. Building on the success of the first edition, this updated collection contains fifty fantastic new spots for 2022. The geographical range of the book is greater than ever before: in particular, we've extended our coverage in Africa to reach the hauntingly beautiful Virunga Mountains in Central Africa and the vibrant West African nation of Senegal. Pore over national parks teeming with wildlife, pulsating cities and jungle-clad mountaintops, and discover crumbling relics of past civilizations and gleaming new monuments.

It's no secret that times have been tough of late for travel, and the world as a whole – shaken to its bones by the coronavirus pandemic. And while it's more important to respect local safety measures and travel sustainably than ever before, all that time spent at home has done much to deepen our appreciation and fuel our wanderlust. In the spirit of escaping the crowds, we've added some great emerging destinations to the list – and we've even been introduced to a couple of spots that we hadn't heard of before. Of the new additions for 2022, we encourage environmentally minded travellers to soak up the *pura vida* in Costa Rica, city-dwellers to inhabit the matchless Euro-Asian culture of Istanbul and intrepid explorers to venture to the bewitching icefields of Greenland.

Throughout the book, you'll find QR codes: scan these for more online information about the relevant destination.

Wherever you dream of going, there's plenty to get excited about in 2022.

ASIA

ASHGABAT

A brand-new city that few people have ever heard of, Ashgabat rises from the ruins of ancient Nisa – capital of the Parthians, who linked Rome with China along the Silk Road. Close by sit the enormous mosque and mausoleum of President Niyazov, who reluctantly steered Turkmenistan from Soviet republic to independent country, with minimal changes. Vast oil and gas revenues boosted the nation's economy and Ashgabat was transformed after Niyazov decreed all buildings must be covered in white marble. Radical designs of most ministry buildings echo their purpose – Telecoms is a massive mobile phone; Publishing is a giant open book; Health is a towering hypodermic needle. Perched precariously between the Iranian mountains and the Karakum Desert, Ashgabat is a remarkable place to visit, but eerily empty. 2021 marked the thirtieth anniversary of Turkmenistan's Independence, with celebrations held on National Carpet Day in May and around October's Independence Day.

The decorative ferris wheel atop Ashgabat's Alem Cultural and Entertainment Center

Türkmenbaşy Ruhy Mosque in Gypjak

A futuristic telephone booth

Russian Bazaar

BAGAN

The Mandalay region of central Myanmar harbours a sight as enchanting as anything in Southeast Asia. The plains of Bagan are scattered with some four thousand ancient temples and pagodas – all that remains of the once-mighty thirteenth- to sixteenth-century Pagan Empire. Why the temples survived while nearly all the secular buildings fell into decay remains a mystery; some have been maintained over the centuries as pilgrimage sites, but many more seem completely deserted. Channelling your inner Indiana Jones as you explore an empty and overgrown temple, with not another soul in sight, is Bagan's great joy. An early morning hot-air balloon ride above the plains, as dawn bathes the temples in pink and their golden stupas glitter in the morning sun, is the stuff that bucket lists are made of – and with Myanmar changing rapidly as it emerges onto the tourist map, chances are it won't be this way forever.

Sulamani Temple

GENGHIS KHAN EQUESTRIAN STATUE

Genghis Khan Equestrian Statue and visitor centre

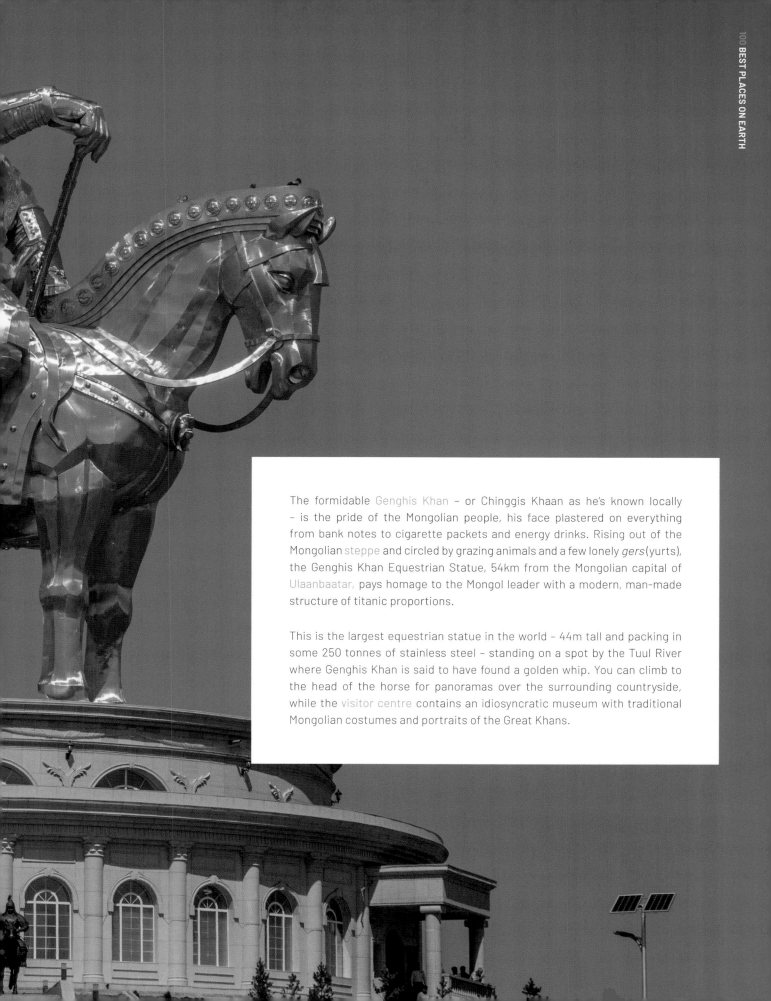

The formidable Genghis Khan – or Chinggis Khaan as he's known locally – is the pride of the Mongolian people, his face plastered on everything from bank notes to cigarette packets and energy drinks. Rising out of the Mongolian steppe and circled by grazing animals and a few lonely *gers* (yurts), the Genghis Khan Equestrian Statue, 54km from the Mongolian capital of Ulaanbaatar, pays homage to the Mongol leader with a modern, man-made structure of titanic proportions.

This is the largest equestrian statue in the world – 44m tall and packing in some 250 tonnes of stainless steel – standing on a spot by the Tuul River where Genghis Khan is said to have found a golden whip. You can climb to the head of the horse for panoramas over the surrounding countryside, while the visitor centre contains an idiosyncratic museum with traditional Mongolian costumes and portraits of the Great Khans.

Jinshanling wall section

GREAT WALL OF CHINA

The practice of building walls along China's northern frontier began in the fifth century BC and continued until the sixteenth century, creating a discontinuous array of fortifications, which came to be known as *Wan Li Changcheng* – "the Great Wall" for English-speakers. Today, the line of the Wall can be followed from Shanhaiguan, by the Yellow Sea, to Jiayuguan in the northwestern deserts, a distance of around 3000km (or, according to a recent survey taking in all the disconnected sections, over 20,000km) – an astonishing featof engineering.

As a symbol of national pride, the Wall's restored sections are besieged daily by tourists, while its image adorns all manner of products, from wine to cigarettes. Yet even the most visited section at Badaling is still easily one of China's most spectacular attractions. Mutianyu is somewhat less crowded, distant Simatai much less so, and far more beautiful. To see the wall in its crumbly glory, head out to Jinshanling, Jiankou or Huanghua, as yet largely untouched by development.

Statues around Juyong Pass

Stretch of wall between Gubeikou and Jinshanling

Great Wall at Jinshanling

Patwon Ki Haveli

JAISALMER

In the remote westernmost corner of Rajasthan, Jaisalmer is the quintessential desert town, its golden, sand-coloured ramparts rearing up from an expanse of scrubby desert like a scene from the *Arabian Nights*.

Jaisalmer's UNESCO-listed Golden Fort sits atop a bluff – its sepia walls slipping from honey to ochre in the setting sun – flanked by tangles of adobe houses. A few thousand inhabitants, dressed in voluminous red and orange turbans, still live within the walls, coming and going through four huge gateways. Seven interlinked Jain temples, dating as far back as the twelfth century, are covered by intricately carved figures and floral latticework.

Traditional townhouses known as *havelis*, built by wealthy eighteenth- and nineteenth-century merchants, line the streets beyond the fort. Many have delicate friezes and overhanging balconies; some are living museums with public access. Jaisalmer is also popular as a base for trips into the Thar Desert, with overnight camel treks to navigate the dunes.

Golden Fort

Moustachioed Jaisalmer resident

Camel ride in the Thar Desert

Jain temple

Hussaini hanging bridge

The Hunza Valley from Baltit Fort

Attabad Lake

Navigating the Karakorum Highway

KARAKORUM HIGHWAY

Carved into the cliffs of one of the world's mightiest mountain ranges along a spellbinding route, the Karakorum Highway is among the world's most exciting overland journeys. There are plenty of bumpy and hair-raising stretches, but massive ongoing upgrades to the road are rendering the trip easier than ever before.

Winding north of the Pakistani plains, the road rises in the foothills, snaking high above the Indus-carved valley as grand vistas unfold, culminating at the junction of the world's three tallest mountain ranges – the Karakorum, the Himalaya and the Hindu Kush. Climbing onward from the regional capital of Gilgit, the road rambles to the border at the Khunjerab – the highest paved pass on earth – but the greatest prize along the route is the mesmerizing Hunza Valley. Home to a diversity of welcoming peoples, long-isolated by the ring of jagged, icy peaks, the vertical landscape is dotted with tranquil villages, hilltop forts, alpine lakes and rickety, wooden foot-bridges – a place where even the longest, most bone-rattling of roads is well worth the journey.

Indian hog deer

KAZIRANGA NATIONAL PARK

First established under the British Raj in 1905 as a protected area offering safe haven to the endangered one-horned rhinoceros, today Kaziranga National Park is home to two-thirds of the world's one-horned rhino population – little wonder it's protected as a World Heritage Site.

Spread across the floodplains of the majestic Brahmaputra River, with the Karbi Anglong Hills lying to the south, its forests, wetlands and grasslands are home to an exotic range of animals, including tigers and elephants, bison and hog deer, and Ganges river dolphins swimming through the park's waters. It is also frequented by a collection of rare migratory birds, while grey pelicans can be seen roosting in nearby villages.

Visitors can see all this on an afternoon jeep safari along the park's rough tracks, safely escorted by a trained armed guard. For the closest sightings, head to the park's Central Range.

Local Majuli man on a wooden boat on the Brahmaputra River

One-horned rhinoceros

Water buffalo

Asian elephant

Infinity pool against the Indian Ocean

Scuba diving around Lhaviyani Atoll

Dinner on the beach

Fresh seafood

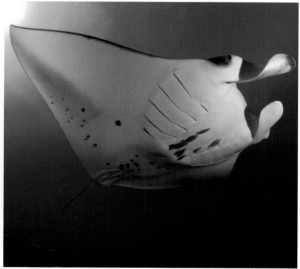
Manta ray

MALDIVES

In the balmy waters of the Indian Ocean, the chain of 26 atolls that makes up the Maldives is synonymous with white-powder beaches, picture-perfect palms and life being lived in the lap of luxury. For once, the tourist clichés are all true: nowhere else on earth will you find such blissful beaches, glassy waters and eye-watering extravagance. Accommodation extends into the ocean on stilts, staffed by Michelin-starred chefs and personal butlers;

you'll also come across an infinity pool lit by twinkling stars, a beachside cinema, and underwater spaces – spas, restaurants, bedrooms and even a nightclub – surrounded by colourful tropical fish.

Marine life is abundant here, and the Maldives supports some of the world's best snorkelling and diving. Multicoloured coral walls and deep caves sustain schools of pretty fish as well as some larger creatures of the deep: manta rays, whale sharks and hammerheads all call the islands their home.

NAGALAND

The jungle-clad hill-state of Nagaland, straddling India's border with Myanmar and home to seventeen distinct tribes, was entirely separate from India until its incorporation into the British Raj. In many ways, it still doesn't feel like India. The state retains a high degree of autonomy, and while foreign visitors can enter freely, Indian citizens still require a special permit.

Headhunting traditions run deep here – the last decapitation as recent as 1963 – most evident in the graphic dances of the Konyaks, reputedly the fiercest of Naga tribes. Visitors can call on former headhunters, now benevolent, aging old men, in their hilltop villages, admire their indigo-ink tattoos evidencing their headhunter status, and share jokes over a cup of thick black tea. Better still, join the December Hornbill Festival, attended by all Nagaland's extraordinarily flamboyant, now largely peace-loving Christian tribes. During the ten-day festivities you'll witness traditional songs, dances and fabulous costumes, and enjoy local foods, sports and the intricate arts and crafts on display around each tribe's unique *morung* (traditional house).

Naga tribal accessories

Performance at the December Hornbill Festival

Verdant landscape at the border of Nagaland

Konyak man in traditional attire

Nyoirin-kannon statue

如意輪観音

Nyoirin-kannon

Looking out from Nigatsu-dō Hall at Tōdaji Temple

Deer roam freely in Nara

Kōfukuji Temple

Nara's 15m Buddha statue

NARA

Nara, the first permanent Japanese capital, is home to no fewer than eight World Heritage sites and continues to play a major role in Japan's cultural legacy. Compact in size and bristling with traditional temples, its most unique attraction and symbol is actually living and breathing. Deer, once considered the messengers of the gods, are protected in Nara today as "Natural Monuments". Follow the pitter-patter of their hooves from Nara Park to one of the most well-known structures in the country, Tōdaji Temple. Completed in 752, it holds great significance for the Japanese. The temple's main feature, Daibutsu-den (Great Buddha Hall), stands as the world's largest wooden building and contains one of Japan's biggest Buddhas. The structure soars at fifteen metres and is cast from some five hundred tonnes of bronze – it is impossible not to be thrown by the grand scale of this treasure.

Ninh Binh landscape

NINH BINH PROVINCE

The scenery in Vietnam's Ninh Binh Province is often described as "Ha Long Bay on Land", but this region is so much more than the famous limestone formations that dot its rice paddies. The lush green fields, atmospheric Buddhist temples and pagodas and grazing water buffalo paint a Vietnamese scene you'll fall instantly in love with. Mua Mountain is one of the highlights of the area; a punishing four hundred steps zigzag upwards to a lookout across the vast karst mountainscape, with spectacular views of Tam Coc village and the Ngo Dong River as it meanders through the endless paddies. You'll be joined at the summit by newlyweds, who climb the mountain in their ivory outfits for the same awe-inspiring wedding photo from the top – you're likely to be as charmed by them as by the dramatic views unfolding before your eyes.

Twilight on Phewa Lake

World Peace Pagoda

Annapurna Base Camp trek

Paragliding above Phewa Lake

Begnas Lake

POKHARA

Most visitors to Pokhara in Nepal will find themselves "Lakeside", and be no the worse for it. Indeed, much of Pokhara's tourist scene is clustered around beautiful Phewa Lake, edged by colourful rowing boats and flanked by wooded mountains. From the shore, the blues and greens of the lake, sky and mountains make for a staggering backdrop, and on clear days long views extend far into the Himalayas – to peaks topping eight thousand metres. If you want similarly awesome surroundings without the tourists, make for Begnas Lake, about 10km to the east.

Relaxed and undemanding, Pokhara makes the perfect launch-pad (or beckoning point of return) for a range of high-octane activities. The Himalayan Annapurna Range is barely 30km to the north and is the setting for a number of world-class treks; rafting and kayaking outfits offer whitewater thrills; while paragliders are well catered for, too. Those in search of less heart-pumping action should try the two-hour climb to the World Peace Pagoda for sweeping views across Pokhara to the unfurling mountains beyond.

Registan Square

Gur-I-Amir mausoleum

Tiger on the Sher-Dor madrassah

Dome of Bibi-Khanum mosque

SAMARKAND

Samarkand, one-time capital of Tamerlane's Silk Road Empire, boasts the region's greatest collection of fourteenth-century Islamic architecture and art. The three madrassahs of Registan Square are an ideal introduction to the perfection and geometrical complexities of Central Asian decorative art, and to myths about forbidden animal and human figures, as seen on the Sher Dor (Lion) madrassah. Wandering through the pleasant pedestrianized streets, glistening blue domes appear around every corner, dominated by the enormous Bibi-Khanum mosque, which tested even Tamerlane's builders. Nearby is the delightful Shah-I-Zinda "Avenue of Tombs", a glazed ceramic riot of every shade of blue imaginable. Tamerlane is buried beneath a stunning turquoise ribbed dome in his own Gur-I-Amir tomb structure – a design style that attained perfection 250 years later with the Taj Mahal. A visual feast, Samarkand still stimulates today and is a highlight of a trip to Uzbekistan.

Intricate Islamic tilework

Jongno District

SEOUL

Operating at a determinedly breakneck speed amid a cartoonish mayhem of lights and sounds, Seoul is like some kind of gigantic, endlessly fascinating pinball machine. Visitors quickly find themselves acclimatizing to the *balli-balli* pace of this high-rise, neon-soaked, open-all-hours city, careening between barbecued meat joints, rice-beer bars and open-air markets as though there weren't enough hours in the day, while racking up bonus points for coping with Korea's famously spicy food. It's also a joy to see the city's other side – palaces, temples, royal tombs and ancestral shrines provide picturesque evidence of Seoul's five centuries as a dynastic capital, and you'll never be far from a mountain to race to the top of. This mix of ancient history and modern-day joie de vivre gives the city an almost unmatched vitality, and the temptation to throw yourself in at the deep end is impossible to resist – Seoul is a city that *really* never sleeps.

Tea plantation, Nuwara Eliya

SRI LANKA

Modest in size compared to many of its Asian neighbours, Sri Lanka packs an astonishing array of attractions into its compact, pearl-shaped outline. The island lies just a few degrees from the equator and boasts an incredibly diverse range of landscapes, from the sultry tropical beaches, coconut plantations and lowland jungles of the coast to the cool green hill country, with its mist-shrouded mountains, crashing waterfalls and boundless tea plantations.

History runs deep in Sri Lanka, and a profusion of ancient monuments commemorates the island's role as one of the great bastions of the Buddhist faith. Massive stupas that rival the pyramids of Egypt in size dot the haunting ruined cities of Anuradhapura and Polonnaruwa, while living Buddhist traditions are evidenced in the vibrant city of Kandy.

Then there are the Sri Lankans themselves. Embroiled for a quarter of a century in one of the world's most pernicious civil wars and traumatized by the devastating 2004 Asian tsunami, and yet they remain among the world's most charming, welcoming and engaging people. Sri Lanka's citizens are happy to share their hard-won peace and growing prosperity with the visitors lucky enough to spend time on their enchanting island.

Traditional dancers in Kandy

Diyaluma Falls

Goyambokka Beach, Tangalle

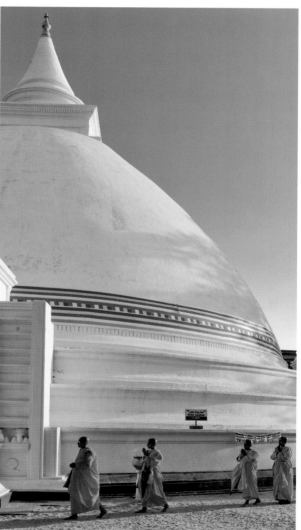

Robed monks, Kelaniya Raja Maha Vihara Temple

TAIWAN

Shaped like a plump teardrop, just south of Japan, is the island of Taiwan. Vastly under the radar, this safe and welcoming country offers vibrant, modern cities; world-class museums and theatres; stunning national parks; scalable snowy peaks; tingling hot-spring resorts; and coastlines that literally take your breath away. Dining out is a national past-time – you'll never go hungry with the ubiquitous nightmarkets winding down past midnight.

The year 2022 marks three years since Taiwan legalized gay marriage – the first and only state in Asia to do so. Yet this progressive and often dramatic democracy still embraces its roots, and native and Chinese cultures can be explored through towering temples, unique cuisines and thrilling festivals. Getting around couldn't be easier: public transport is efficient and cheap and people are famously kind and helpful. Life is so good here that many tourists never leave, choosing Taiwan for their new home.

Longshan Temple in Taipei

Fabrika – a multifunctional space set inside an old sewing factory

Rhike Park

Tbilisi National Gallery

Enjoying the sunshine

TBILISI

While the Georgian capital, Tbilisi, has long lured visionary types to its bohemian neighbourhoods, it's slipped under the tourist radar for years. That may have something to do with its turbulent recent history: although Georgia gained independence from the Soviet Union in 1991, there followed a period of civil war, violence and ethnic tensions.

Over the past decade, however, a new generation has reignited Tbilisi's cultural scene through a mix of local art galleries, exhibition spaces, music venues, concept stores and creative hubs. A growing crop of industrial-style hotels is springing up across the city, many set in Soviet-era factories and publishing houses. The food scene is thriving, too – innovative chefs have taken the helm in the kitchens of new restaurants, where they reimagine traditional Georgian cuisine with a modern twist. The revolution is underway.

Bridge of Peace

Huge stone face at Angkor Thom

View over Angkor Wat

Bas-relief depiction of King Suryavarman II at Angkor Wat

Monk at Ta Prohm

TEMPLES OF ANGKOR

The world-famous temples of Angkor dot the Cambodian countryside, rising out of the enveloping forest like the classic lost-in-the-jungle ancient ruins of every Hollywood filmmaker's wildest dreams. Top of most visitors' lists is the unforgettable Angkor Wat, with its five soaring towers hemmed in by a moat. The surreal Bayon, plastered with hundreds of superhuman faces, and the jungle temple of Ta Prohm, its crumbling ruins clamped in the grip of giant kapok trees, are also must-sees.

However many times you've seen it on film or in photographs, nothing readies you for the majesty of Angkor Wat. Dominated by five majestic, corncob towers, this masterpiece of Khmer architecture was built by Suryavarman II between around 1113 and 1150. Stunning from a distance, its intricacy becomes apparent as you approach, with every surface covered in fine detail. Throughout the day the colour of its stone changes with the light.

TIP OF BORNEO

In the compact state of Sabah, most first-time travellers to Borneo follow the well-trodden route between Kinabalu, Kinabatangan and the Sandakan islands to get a glimpse of unique and endangered species, most famously the orangutan. But to get truly "off the beaten path" and to discover the other fascinating inhabitants of Sabah, head to the northernmost part of the island, the Tip of Borneo.

Known locally as Tanjung Sipang Mengayu, this windswept promontory between the South China and Sulu seas offers dreamlike sunsets, sandy beaches, rugged rainforests and the best surf in Malaysia. It is here, in the rural area about 40km from Kudat, that a community of traditional Rungus people reside. Spend a couple of days exploring the area, discovering Rungus villages, inquisitive locals and unspoilt beaches (which you're likely to get all to yourself). Environmentally minded travellers will want to consider staying in a local ecolodge.

The South China and Sulu seas meet at the Tip of Borneo

Looking down over Tun Sakaran Marine Park

Rungus girl in traditional attire

Female orangutan with her infant

TOKYO

Tokyo is exactly what you think it is, and nothing like you expect. It is kimono-clad women stepping daintily along Asakusa streets, neon signs jostling for attention, white-gloved station attendants squeezing commuters into subway cars. It is narrow alleyways strung with a tangle of overhead cables, neighbourhood shrines with offerings of beer and satsumas, processions of schoolchildren with identical backpacks. Iconic activities range from sushi to sumo, geisha to gardens, neon to noodles. Ordered yet bewildering, Japan's pulsating capital will lead you a merry dance: this is Asia at its weirdest, straightest, prettiest, sleaziest and coolest, all at the same time.

With the 2020 Olympics delayed to 2021 because of the ongoing coronavirus pandemic, the eyes of the world have remained on Tokyo, the largest city to ever host the games.

Shinjuku Gyoen Garden

Sushi from Tsukiji Fish Market

Japanese sumo wrestlers

Shinjuku alleyway

Kimono-clad Tokyoite

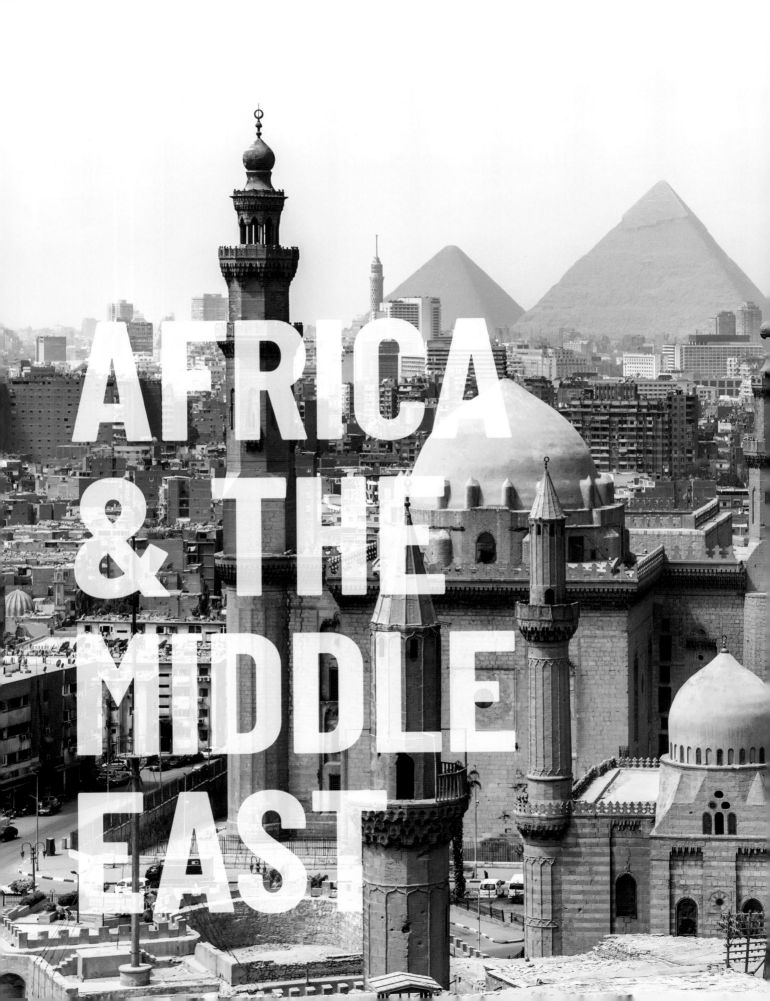

AFRICA
& THE
MIDDLE
EAST

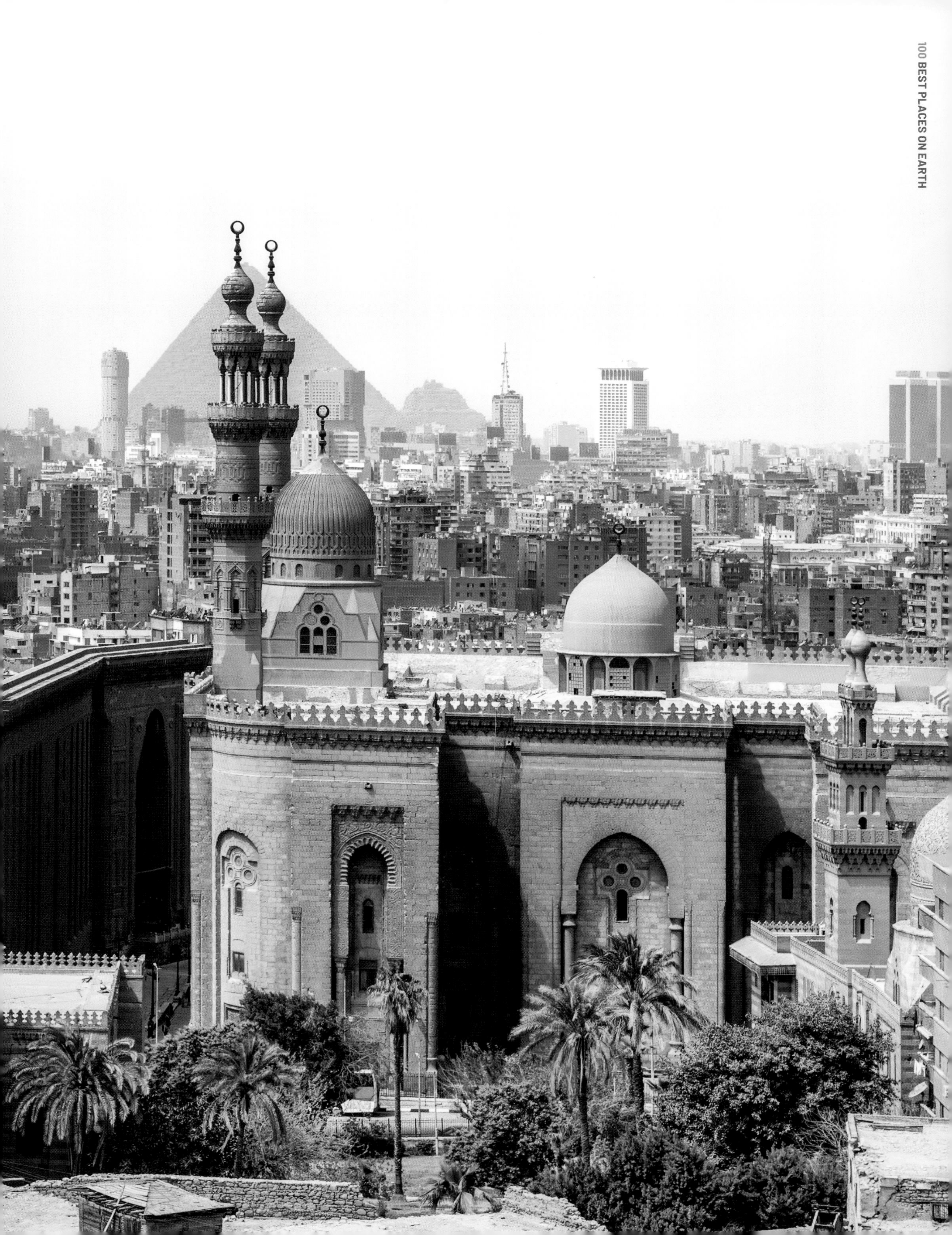

DUBAI

Dubai is like nowhere else on the planet. Often claimed to be the world's fastest-growing city, in the past four decades it has metamorphosed from a small Gulf trading centre to become one of the world's most glamorous, spectacular and futuristic urban destinations, fuelled by a heady cocktail of petrodollars, visionary commercial acumen and naked ambition. Dubai's ability to dream – and then achieve – the impossible has ripped up expectations and rewritten the record books, as evidenced by stunning developments such as the soaring Burj Khalifa, the beautiful Burj al Arab, the vast Palm Jumeirah island and the world's largest single-site solar park, which covers a staggering 77 square kilometres. Each is a remarkable testament to the ruling sheikh's determination to make this one of the world's essential destinations for the twenty-first century.

High glamour, high rise and high tech, this hypermodern oasis makes a fitting setting for the delayed 2020 World Expo, replanned for October 2021 to March 2022 in the wake of coronavirus.

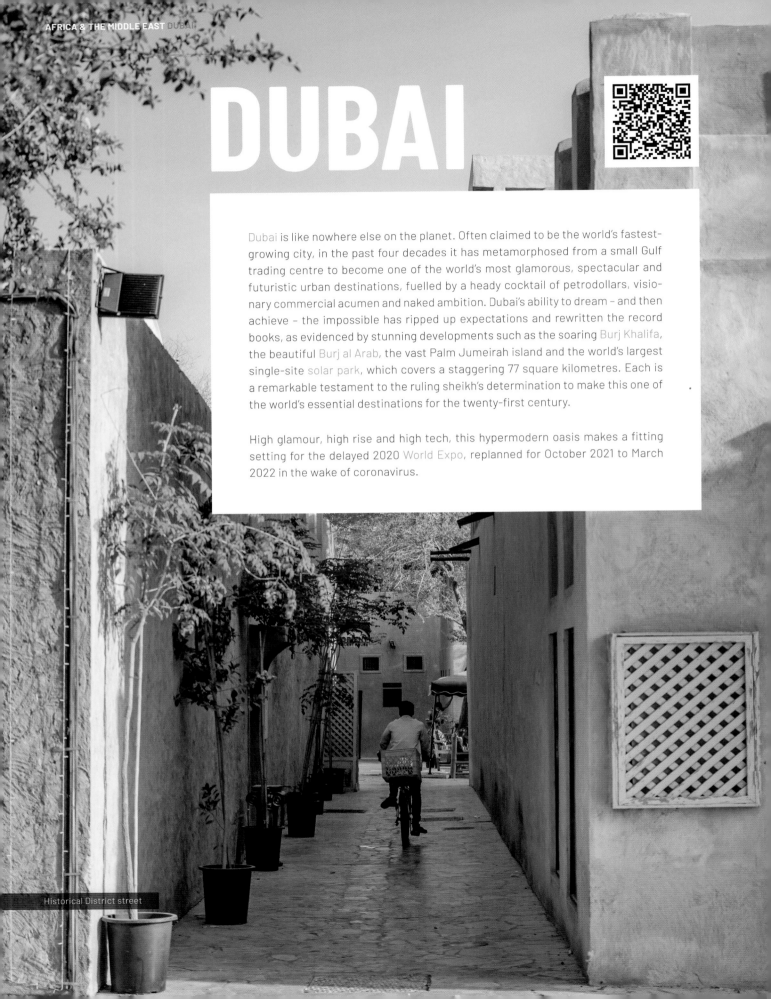

Historical District street

Dubai skyline

Museum of the Poet Al Oqaili

Inside the Old Fort

Celebrating Timkat festival

ETHIOPIA

An enigmatic and utterly beguiling country, Ethiopia has endless intrigue. From its unique, highly sociable cuisine – the basis of which is *injera*, a spongy sour-dough pancake, piled high with piquant curries and stews and shared between friends – to its ancient language and curly Amharic script, there's very little that's familiar about this place, and it's all the better for it.

Ethiopia is a largely Orthodox Christian country, and its religious festivals and structures are something to behold. The sunken churches of Lalibela, hand-carved out of red rock below ground some nine hundred years ago, are an astonishing feat of engineering. Come January, the network of tunnels and staircases that connect all eleven fill up with thousands of worshippers dressed in white, celebrating the birth of Christ with a twelve-hour mass.

Elsewhere, you'll discover castles dating back to the sixteenth century, a curious coffee culture and an Ethio-jazz scene in the capital Addis Ababa like no other.

Traditional Ethiopian coffee ceremony

Illustrated Amharic bible

Rock-hewn Church of St George, Lalibela

Ethiopian spread

University of al-Qarawiyyin

Walking through Fez medina

Shops lining the medina streets

Al-Attarine madrassa

FEZ

The shrill cry of a market seller, the trot of a donkey's hooves, the rush of fiery harissa invading your nostrils and a young man dunking a sheet of leather into a heavy pot of henna at the Chouara Tanneries – the sounds, smells and sights of the Fez medina never end. Nine thousand alleys make up this labyrinthine UNESCO-listed site, where only wandering feet can explore and get lost down its twists and turns. A car-free area, the medina's footprint hasn't altered in close to a millennium. Home to the oldest university in the world, infinite hole-in-the-wall food joints and majestic tiled entrances, Fez's traditions and allure both endure.

Chouara Tanneries

IRAN

Iran is a land shrouded in mystery. Look beyond the headlines and you'll get a clearer sense of this captivating country, which packs endless rewards and tremendous surprises into its borders. Filled with fascinating landmarks – the Achaemenid's former capital, Persepolis; striking structures from the Qajar dynasty like Golestan Palace; and umpteen grand squares, most notably Naqsh-e Jahan – Iran ticks all the boxes. But Iran is much more than a list of sights to see. It's the experiences that provide the real tales: watching elderly men weight-training to the beat of a drum in an ancient gym, zipping down the smooth slopes of the Alborz Mountains, meeting friendly nomads while hiking, and receiving heartfelt invitations for tea. For it's these encounters that travellers frequently find the most enriching, touched by Iran's enduring hospitality and surprised to find a country so different from its contentious international reputation.

The Golestan Palace and fountains

JEBEL SAHRO

Trekking amongst the bizarre rock formations of the Jebel Sahro, an arid mountain chain in southern Morocco, can feel like walking on the moon. You won't meet many people here other than transhumance Aït 'Atta Berbers: the women dressed gaudily, bedecked in bright, heavy jewellery, fashioned from semi-precious stones and silver coins, baking bread on red-hot ashes buried in the earth, bearded men sporting turbans, ornate daggers at their side. Many still live in traditional black goat-hair tents, alongside their camels and sheep.

Gather around a crackling fire under a starry night sky, share stories, listen to drumming and traditional songs recounting folkloric tales of a heroic, bygone age, reverberating around the black mountainside. Better still, join a family on their annual springtime migration, an epic twelve-day trek heading northwards for their summer pastures in the High Atlas, or otherwise the return in autumn to their southerly Jebel Sahro homeland before winter sets in.

Looking out over the Jebel Sahro

Moroccan Berber donning traditional clothes

Berber village in the Jebel Sahro

Trekking in the mountains

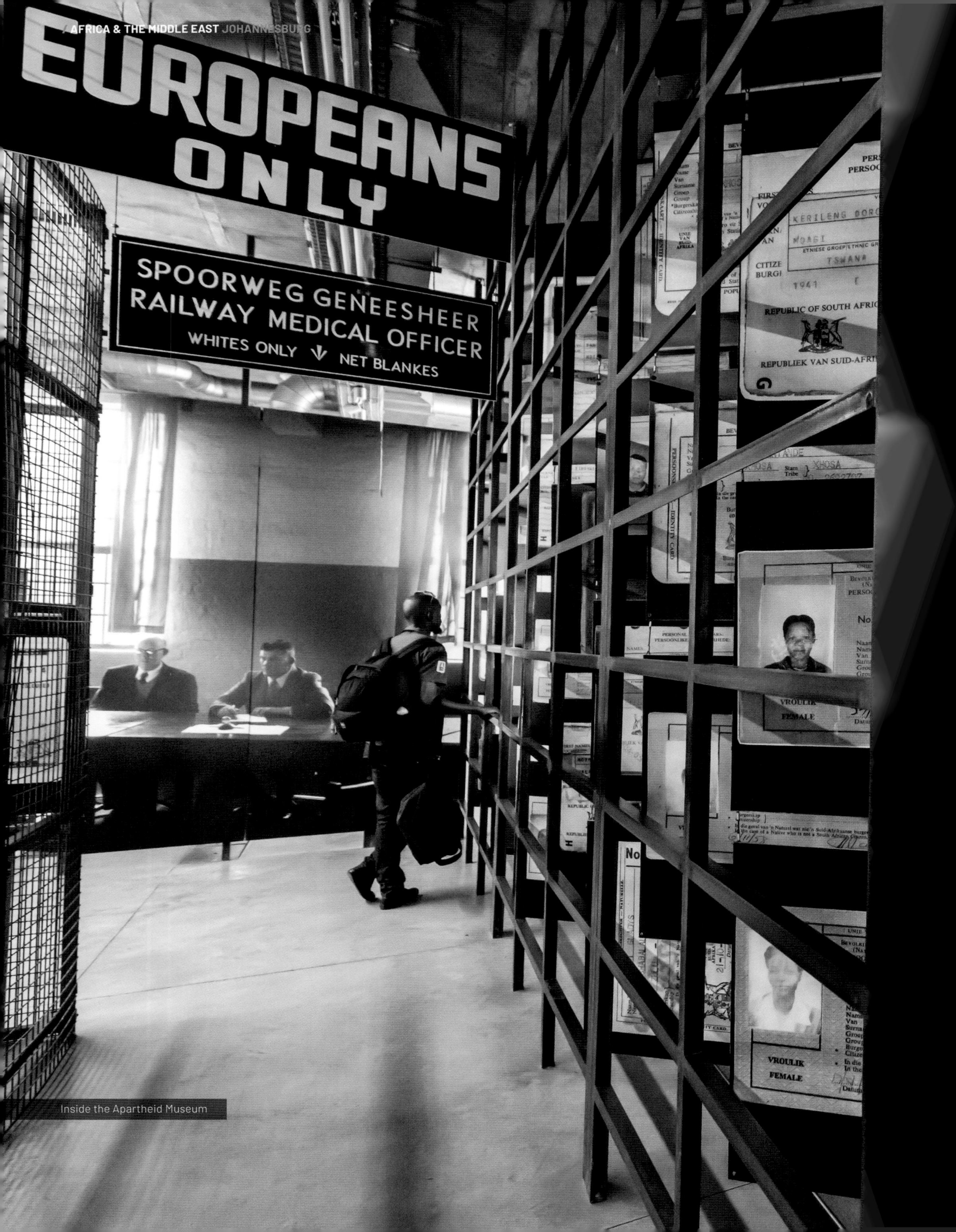

EUROPEANS ONLY

SPOORWEG GENEESHEER
RAILWAY MEDICAL OFFICER
WHITES ONLY ↓ NET BLANKES

Inside the Apartheid Museum

Woman and child in a Joburg slum

Selling oysters and wine at the Neighbourgoods Market

Colourful craft necklaces for sale in Maboneng

The Cradle of Humankind

JOHANNESBURG

In 1884, vast quantities of gold were found below remote farms on the Highveld plateau in South Africa. Ten years later, a city of 100,000 had grown, its inhabitants drawn from across the world. The pioneering spirit of Johannesburg still survives, and this sprawling metropolis of 5.5 million is now Africa's most cosmopolitan city, where great wealth sits beside deep poverty, and where most people come from somewhere else. It's surprisingly easy for visitors to get to know Joburg and its mostly harmless inhabitants; following simple safety rules should keep you out of any trouble. A decade of regeneration and investment has transformed parts of the city centre, where new museums, ultra-cool hotels and hostels have opened. The weekend markets in Braamfontein and Maboneng are great for sampling African cuisine, shopping for art, crafts and souvenirs and mingling with the locals. Jaw-dropping views can be had from the 225-metre-high Carlton Tower, or on a tour of Hillbrow and the remarkable Ponte City skyscraper. Further afield, boutique shopping centres, the Apartheid Museum, bicycle tours of Soweto and a trip to the Cradle of Humankind – finding place of many early hominid fossils – are unmissable. End your visit on a high with sundowners at a classy spot in the northern suburbs.

A dhow off the coast of Lamu

LAMU

An important centre of maritime trade since medieval times, the island-bound port-town of Lamu has a rich and chequered history, a captivating architectural heritage and a vibrant cultural identity unmatched by any other settlement along the Swahili Coast of East Africa.

The Old Town – comprising a labyrinth of whitewashed traditional two- and three-storey buildings – rises in isolation from the surrounding coastal scrub. There's no industrial development or modern suburbia in sight, nor is there any significant division between residential and business districts. Private homes, hotels, restaurants, mosques and shops jostle for space along shady, cobbled alleys, where children play unsupervised, old men sit gossiping, veiled women look out from carved wooden doorways, and donkeys – the island's main form of transport – plod past, occasionally shattering the peace with a heartfelt bray.

At once impenetrably anachronistic and oddly cosmopolitan, Lamu's alleys lend themselves to unstructured exploration on foot. The surrounding archipelago also offers plenty of worthwhile excursions, be it a gentle waterfront stroll to idyllic Shela Beach, snorkelling the reefs from a local dhow, or the adventurous crossing to Pate Island, whose trio of absorbingly time-warped small towns – Faza, Situ and Pate itself – make Lamu seem positively urbane.

Lamu street life

A donkey passes through Lamu Old Town

Shela Beach

Riyadha mosque

LESOTHO

Against all odds, the plucky, landlocked kingdom of Lesotho managed to stay independent despite South Africa's tight embrace, leaving much of its highland village culture intact and making it a delight to explore today. Most of Lesotho is mountainous, with peaks up to 3500 metres, and its lowest point, at 1400 metres above sea level, is the highest "low point" of any country in the world. The remote highlands offer hiking and camping in wild national parks, but for a less taxing introduction to the country, visit the lodges at Malealea or Semongkong, former trading posts, for well-organized pony treks to see local villages, gaping gorges and tumbling waterfalls. Nearby, Morija has a museum and art centre, as well as some of Lesotho's disturbingly large fossilized dinosaur footprints, dating back some two hundred million years. New roads cross the interior, making it easier than ever to reach the grand 185-metre-high Katse Dam for an inland tour, while 4WD enthusiasts can attempt crossing into South Africa via the spectacular hairpins of Sani Pass. Take it slowly to get the most out of a visit and remember to look up at night – low light pollution and clear skies in Lesotho make for fabulous stargazing.

Maletsunyane River Valley

Women in Antananarivo

Manual pollination of vanilla

Chameleon in Andasibe National Park

Ring-tailed lemur

MADAGASCAR

Madagascar is like nowhere else on earth. Set adrift in the middle of the Indian Ocean about 500km from Africa and almost ten times as distant from Asia, it is the world's fourth-largest island and the most isolated landmass of comparable proportions anywhere in the tropics. Culturally and ethnically, the Malagasy people have diverse origins, essentially being a fusion of Indonesian and African stock, but once liberally spiced with influences from Arabia, India, China, France and elsewhere.

For many visitors, the primary attraction of the island is its postcard-perfect beaches, turquoise lagoons, whispering palm plantations, craggy islets and snorkel-friendly coral reefs that adorn its 10,000km coastline. For adventurous travellers, however, Madagascar really comes into its own away from the beaches. This immense tropical island is sometimes referred to as the Eighth Continent on account of its unique biodiversity, which incorporates an estimated ten thousand animal and plant species found nowhere else in the world. Now protected in a network of roughly fifty official national parks and reserves, this diversity includes one hundred species of loveable lemur, and a similar tally of colourful chameleons and endemic birds.

PETRA

Petra astounds. Tucked away in a remote valley basin in the heart of southern Jordan's Shara mountains and shielded from the outside world behind an impenetrable barrier of rock, this ancient city remains wreathed in mystery. Today, it's as if time has literally drawn a veil over Petra, which grew wealthy enough on the caravan trade to challenge the might of Rome: two millennia of wind and rain have blurred the sharp edges of its ornate Classical facades and rubbed away at its soft sandstone to expose vivid bands of colour beneath, putting the whole scene into soft focus.

The arrival never disappoints. The epic walk in, down the wadi and into the twisting narrow gorge known as the Siq, precedes an initial glimpse of the sunlit Treasury which is as jaw-dropping as when Burckhardt "rediscovered" Petra over two hundred years ago. Smoothly eroded Nabataean tombs, with their swirling layers of multicoloured sandstone, imperiously dominate the later Roman Theatre. Walk along the Colonnaded Street then tackle the stepped climb to the remarkable rock-cut Monastery, carved from the mountain summit. Be prepared to have your imagination fired.

Approaching the Treasury

Camel in front of the Pyramids of Giza

PYRAMIDS OF GIZA

Instantly familiar yet consistently awe-inspiring, the Pyramids of Giza are the last of the Seven Wonders of the Ancient World to have survived the ravages of time. Erupting from the edge of the Western Desert, they are part of a larger complex that includes the Great Sphinx, a collection of smaller pyramids, cemeteries, temples and an ancient workers' village. The compelling Egyptian capital, Cairo, creeps closer every year and fantastic new views of the city and the pyramids will soon emerge from the top levels of the brand new Grand Egyptian Museum – originally scheduled to open in 2020 but pushed back to 2021 by the coronavirus pandemic. This oasis of culture in the desert, only two kilometres away from the Pharaonic necropolis, is set to be the biggest archeological museum in the world. It will house around 100,000 artefacts, including 5400 belonging to Tutankhamun, displayed together for the very first time since King Tut took what he thought would be his final resting place.

SAHARA DESERT

The Sahara Desert conjures a string of romantic images: swirling sands, covered-up Bedouin, mirages, thirsty caravans stumbling upon an oasis set amid swaying palms. While little of this vision has any foundation in reality – the caravans have all but vanished and the Bedouin have traded their camels for Toyotas – not even the vestiges of modern humanity are capable of taming this majestic wilderness, where shifting sands can block roads for days and where the foolhardy can still meet death by the sting of a scorpion.

The Sahara spreads out across North Africa, covering an area of staggering proportions – 9,400,000 square kilometres and growing – hemmed in by the Atlas Mountains and the Mediterranean to the north, the Red Sea in the east, the Sahel in the south and the Atlantic in the west. The world's greatest expanse of desert is broken only by dots of green, where human habitation has survived the spread of sands, and temporary camps where Bedouin communities gather around their campfires. It is hard to overstate the scale and splendour of the desert, where the space, the sky and the silence are all colossal – and where the stark landscape and its hardy inhabitants continue to withstand the sands of time.

Night sky over the Sahara

Camel trekking

Desert scorpion

Berber musician

Wolof woman

Saly seaside resort

Blue-shuttered colonial house in Saint Louis

Bungalows in Cap Skirring

SENEGAL

With sweeping grasslands, dense rainforest and a North Atlantic coastline, Senegal is a hugely diverse country, as well as being one of the most stable in Africa. Known as the "Gateway to Africa", it's not short on cultural influences, either. French is the official language, but Wolof culture is prominent too (Wolof remains the most widely spoken language), and at one time or another the British, Dutch and Portuguese all laid claim to parts of the nation.

The capital, Dakar, is the beating heart of Senegal. It brims with markets, throbs with music and serves up tantalizing food (local dishes like thiebou-dieune are not to be missed), while the neighbourhoods of Yoff, Ouakam and Île de N'Gor are a surfer's paradise. Along the west coast, you'll find a natural beach crawl in the Petite Côte and Cap Skirring; to the east, rivers wend through national parks heavy with wildlife (though if you're looking for the Big Five, it's advisable to head elsewhere in Africa). To the north, meanwhile, Saint-Louis' wealth of fading colonial architecture infuses the city with an understated charm.

Sharing a dish of thieboudieune

SERENGETI NATIONAL PARK

Tanzania's Serengeti National Park is arguably the finest safari destination anywhere in Africa. The centrepiece of an unfenced cross-border ecosystem that extends across 40,000 square kilometres, this immense park is almost without equal for carnivores. Blonde-maned lions lounge nonchalantly in the shade, solitary cheetahs pace the open plains, spotted hyenas lope and sniff around their subterranean dens, and leopards bask in the umbrella-thorn acacias that line the Seronera River.

Serengeti is best known for the annual migration of up to two million wildebeest that traverses its plains. Wildlife viewing throughout the park is fantastic all year round, but there are seasonal and regional highlights. These include the February calving season, when thousands of newborns drop daily, attracting hordes of opportunistic predators to the southern plains, and the adrenaline-charged river crossings, usually comprising thousands of individual wildebeest, that occur in the far north between August and November.

Some complain that the park's popular Seronera circuit becomes overrun with safari jeeps. True enough, but this ignores the fact that the Serengeti is a seriously vast place. Head out further afield and the horizonless oceans of grass, standing tall and green after the rains, more cropped and yellow in the dry season, still evoke the soul-stirring sense of space alluded to in the Maasai word (*Siringit*, meaning "Endless Plain") from which the park's name derives.

Zebra crossing

VICTORIA FALLS

Along with Mount Everest and the Grand Canyon, Victoria Falls – or Mosi-oa-Tunya ("the smoke that thunders") – ranks as one of the world's seven natural wonders. No matter how many pictures you've seen beforehand, nothing can prepare you for the awe-inspiring sight and deafening sound of the falls. The world's widest curtain of water crashes down a huge precipice, producing clouds of spray visible from afar, before squeezing into a zigzag of sheer-sided gorges as a torrent of turbulent rapids, carving its way to the Indian Ocean well over 1000km away.

Their dramatic setting on the Zambezi river – on the Zambia-Zimbabwe border – has also made Victoria Falls the undisputed adventure capital of Africa. There's an array of adrenaline-fuelled activities on offer, from whitewater rafting and bungee jumping to zip-lining and bodyboarding. Less touted are the stunning wildlife-viewing opportunities Victoria Falls affords: the national parks that line the serene banks of the Upper Zambezi are home to large mammals, such as elephant, lion, buffalo, giraffe and leopard, as well as a variety of antelope and more than 410 bird species.

Trees peering over Victoria Falls

VIRUNGA MOUNTAINS

Bubbling lava lakes, towering bamboo cathedrals and tangled rainforests are just some of the landscapes protected in the Virunga Mountains, a staggeringly beautiful string of nine freestanding volcanoes that rises to 4507 metres on the border of Rwanda, Uganda and the Democratic Republic of Congo.

The Virungas are home to more than half the world's mountain gorillas. Staring into the deep brown eyes of one of these gentle giants – no taller than the average human, but more than twice as bulky – ranks among the world's most exhilarating and emotionally charged wildlife encounters.

Other wildlife includes secretive buffalos and elephants, bamboo-guzzling golden monkeys, and dozens of colourful highland bird species. For fit and energetic travellers, the steep volcanic slopes incorporate some stupendous hiking goals: be it the 4507-metre peak of Karisimbi, the fire-spitting cauldron of lava enclosed by the 3470-metre rim of Nyiragongo, or the gorgeous crater lake that caps the 3711-metre Bisoke.

The Virungas reflected in Lake Mutanda

Lava in Nyiragongo's crater

Hiking to Nyiragongo through the rainforest

Mountain gorilla

EUROPE

The Acropolis

ACROPOLIS

The rock of the Acropolis, crowned by the dramatic ruins of the Parthenon, is one of the archetypal images of Western culture. The first time you see it, rising above the traffic or from a distant hill, is extraordinary: foreign, and yet utterly familiar. As in other Greek cities, the Acropolis itself is simply the highest point of Athens, and this steep-sided, flat-topped crag of limestone, rising abruptly 100m from its surroundings, has made it the focus of the city during every phase of its development. Easily defensible and with plentiful water, its initial attractions are obvious – little wonder it served as home to one of the earliest known settlements in Greece in 5000 BC. Even now, with no function apart from tourism, the Acropolis is the undeniable heart of the city, around which everything else clusters, glimpsed at every turn.

Frieze on the Parthenon

Amphitheatre of the Acropolis

Acropolis at sunset

Erechtheum at the Acropolis

Fortress in Gjirokastra

Lake Koman

Walking in the Albanian Alps

Bunk'Art, Tirana

People gathered for the opening ceremony of Tirana's Skanderbeg Square

ALBANIA

The perfect destination for adventurous travellers, Albania packs a huge variety of sights and affordable experiences into a relatively small area. Inhabited by disarmingly friendly locals, this Balkan nation has a surprising history of religious tolerance. Start with the capital, Tirana, renowned for its lively nightlife and the excellent Bunk'Art museum housed in a former nuclear bunker, then make for Berat and Gjirokastra, beautifully preserved Ottoman-era towns with hilltop castles and cobblestone alleys. In the south, barren mountains plunge down to the Mediterranean Sea, where you'll find pebble beaches backed by fragrant olive and citrus groves, the atmospheric ruins of ancient Butrint and the last untamed river in Europe. Near charming Korça, explore the frescoed monasteries of Voskopoja, go pelican-spotting or hike around Dhardha village. In the north, the stunning Albanian Alps offer dramatic hiking, village homestays and the scenic Lake Koman ferry ride. The winding roads and erratic local driving habits make the going slow – but this is a country worth savouring.

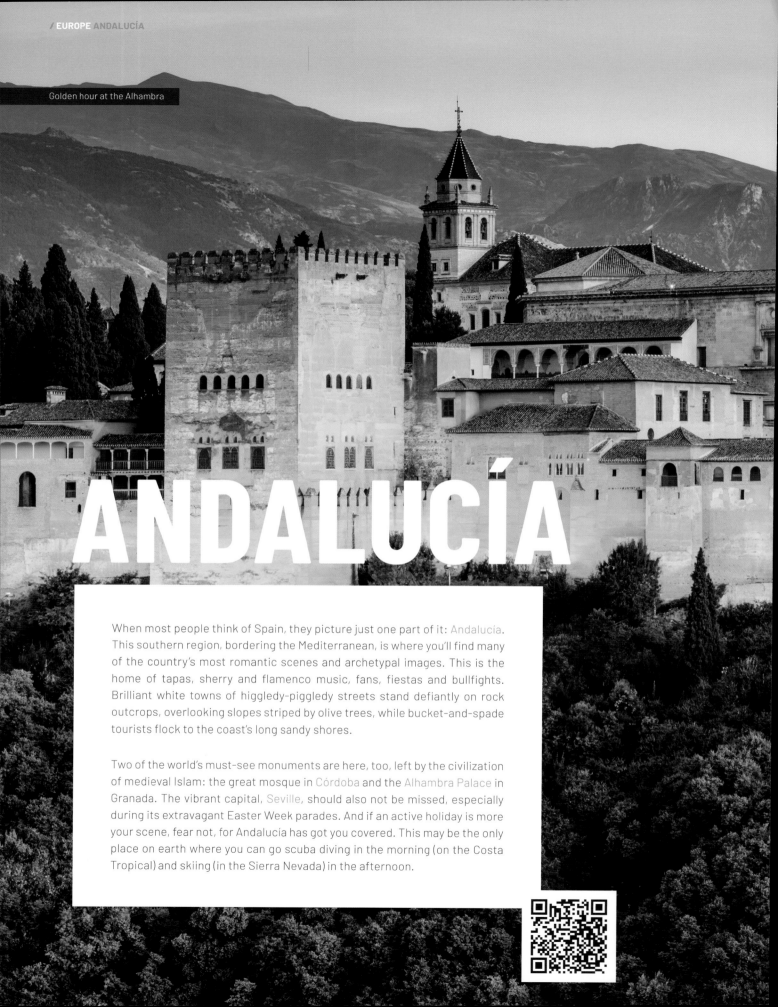

Golden hour at the Alhambra

ANDALUCÍA

When most people think of Spain, they picture just one part of it: Andalucía. This southern region, bordering the Mediterranean, is where you'll find many of the country's most romantic scenes and archetypal images. This is the home of tapas, sherry and flamenco music, fans, fiestas and bullfights. Brilliant white towns of higgledy-piggledy streets stand defiantly on rock outcrops, overlooking slopes striped by olive trees, while bucket-and-spade tourists flock to the coast's long sandy shores.

Two of the world's must-see monuments are here, too, left by the civilization of medieval Islam: the great mosque in Córdoba and the Alhambra Palace in Granada. The vibrant capital, Seville, should also not be missed, especially during its extravagant Easter Week parades. And if an active holiday is more your scene, fear not, for Andalucía has got you covered. This may be the only place on earth where you can go scuba diving in the morning (on the Costa Tropical) and skiing (in the Sierra Nevada) in the afternoon.

Calahonda on the Costa Tropical

Cured serrano-ham tapas

Easter in Seville

Moorish columns in the Prayer Hall, Mosque–Cathedral of Córdoba

Lagoa das Furnas, São Miguel

Sperm whale-tail fin with Mount Pico in the background

Cow standing in a lake by Mount Pico on Pico Island

Fumaroles are scattered around the village of Furnas

AZORES

Few people know much about the Azores as a travel destination. But this remote Portuguese archipelago in the middle of the Atlantic is starting to be recognized as an active, nature-lover's paradise. The nine volcanic islands offer visitors a world of dazzling blue lakes fringed by green forests; blistering thermal springs and fumaroles; mystical grottoes formed by molten rock;

and calderas flanked by dramatic mountainscapes. The mighty Atlantic waters surrounding the islands play home to a third of the world's cetaceans, including bottlenose dolphins, sperm whales and, on occasion, blue whales.

With scenery not dissimilar to that of New Zealand or Bolivia, and the traditional cuisine and culture of Portugal, the Azores offer active travellers the whole package. The enchanting island group is one to watch in 2022.

Exploring a cave in the Azores

BAUTZEN

With a tenth-century castle, cobbled streets and stone towers capping the skyline, the medieval centre of Bautzen looks as if it were plucked from a fairy-tale. This hilltop town on Saxony's River Spree has a charming, quirky character, reflected in attractions including a leaning tower, a mustard museum and even a dinosaur park. But Bautzen has a darker side, too. Home to two notorious prisons during the Nazi and Soviet eras, the city has emerged from a chequered past – learn more by joining a tour of Bautzen II, which became East Germany's most infamous Stasi prison.

What really sets Bautzen apart, though, is its status as the cultural capital of the smallest Slavic group in the world – the Sorbs. Around ten percent of the city's population are of Sorbian nationality and their influence is keenly felt. All street signs are bilingual and you'll find a Sorbian restaurant, museum and theatre, while age-old traditions and customs are alive and well. The annual procession of Easter Riders is particularly enchanting, when Sorbian men dress in all their finery and ride through town on decorated horses, singing traditional Sorbian hymns.

Bautzen's historic Old Town

Sorbian Easter riders and spectators during the Easter procession

Medieval city street

Exhibit inside Bautzen II

Berlin nightlife

Gedenkstätte Berliner Mauer

Street art

The fall of the wall, November 9, 1989

BERLIN WALL

The scenes of August 13, 1961, when Berlin was cut in two, are still vivid in many people's minds. Literally overnight, not only were capitalism and communism divided, but families too. To Erich Honecker's East German regime, it was an "anti-Fascist protective wall"; to the rest of the world, it was a symbol of oppression.

The Berlin Wall, landmark of a divided city, finally fell on November 9, 1989, and East and West Berliners celebrated together for the first time in 28 years. The wall now belongs to history – although parts can still be seen. At the East Side Gallery in Friedrichshain, a 1.3km surviving stretch has been covered in political and satirical murals painted by artists from all over the world, while at the Gedenkstätte Berliner Mauer a 60m section of the Wall still stands in all its frightening might, together with a centre that keeps the story of the Wall alive using photos, sound recordings and information terminals.

In Berlin today there is hardly a trace of the old border crossings, yet nowhere else in Germany are the consequences of reunification felt so strongly. The city's 1989 rebirth is key to understanding Berlin's youthful vitality. The first wave of *post-Wende* ("turning-point") settlers – artists, squatters, musicians, DJs – set the edgy, alternative tone that still drives the city today.

CAPPADOCIA

Forged by wind and water, the otherworldly terrain of Cappadocia has long been one of Turkey's star attractions, its soft, volcanic rock contoured by the elements over millennia into cones, mushrooms and pillars. Its hills are dotted with fantastical forms, honeycombed with cavern towns – best taken in on a hot-air balloon ride after bedding down in a rockhewn hotel. The landscape around the sleepy town of Göreme is particularly spectacular, peppered with "fairy chimneys" and dotted with cave churches adorned with Byzantine frescoes.

From around the fourth century AD, Christians carved a labyrinth of cave dwellings and tunnels into, and beneath, the stone – some dug eighteen levels deep. Dozens of their vast subterranean towns have been found, most famously the sprawling complexes of Derinkuyu and Kaymaklı, linked by an 8km tunnel. Believed to be larger still is the more recently discovered labyrinth beneath the citadel of Nevşehir, the excavated upper reaches of which were opened in 2020.

Uchisar Castle, Cappadocia

Stradun

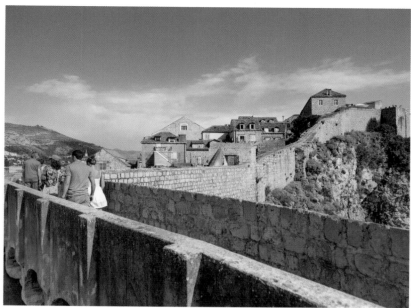
Dubrovnik city walls

Old Town and port

Pile Gate

Dubrovnik's iconic red roofs

DUBROVNIK OLD TOWN

A walled, sea-battered city lying at the foot of a grizzled mountain, Dubrovnik is Croatia's most popular tourist destination, and it's not difficult to see why. An essentially medieval town reshaped by Baroque planners after the earthquake of 1667, Dubrovnik's historic core seems to have been suspended in time ever since. A labyrinth of tiny cobbled alleyways inside the Old Town gives way to bougainvillea-draped limestone buildings, housing a variety of restaurants and shops. One main thoroughfare runs through the melee: Stradun leads from Pile Gate, the main entrance to the city, to the Old Town Harbour, where ferries lead to lush islands just off shore.

The original city walls date back to the eighth century; modified and extended over the years, they now stand 25m high and stretch for some 2km. The walls are encrusted with towers and bastions, and it's impossible not to be struck by their remarkable size and state of preservation. Once you're on top, endless views extend over the mass of red-tiled roofs, the deep-blue Adriatic and the arid face of Srđ Mountain.

The Quays

Kirwan's Lane

The Galway coast

Wild oysters

GALWAY

The delightful harbour city of Galway in western Ireland is a vibrant, fun-loving place known for its festivals, music and bars. Its town centre is compact and colourful, its cobbled streets lined with buskers who sing for their supper, atmospheric old buildings and traditional pubs ringing with live Irish music and good *craic*.

Medieval remnants such as the old city walls, the Spanish Arch and stone facades fronting artsy boutiques make a perfect backdrop for Galway's laidback, bohemian atmosphere. There's a passionate local food scene too, from cosy cafés, bistros and fine-dining restaurants to the delectable week-end market and September oyster festival. Make for Salthill to stroll along the seaside promenade fronting Galway Bay.

As the capital of the Gaelic West, this is the only city in the country where you might possibly hear Irish spoken on the streets. Galway also lies on the Wild Atlantic Way, making it the perfect jumping-off point for exploring the remote peninsulas of Connaught and Connemara, with their rugged shores, lochs and mountains.

GREENLAND

Despite its name, the Danish territory of Greenland is not the place to come for lush forests or woodland frolics. What it lacks in green, however, the world's largest island makes up for in sublime wintry beauty. Its towering icebergs and glaciers are bewitching, their stark white hardness edged by soft blue wisps.

Greenland is the ideal destination to tick a cluster of winter adventures off your list, from seeing the Northern Lights emblazoned across the sky to being tugged along on a dogsled, basking in the Scandinavian midnight sun or kayaking among the fjords. In cities such as Nuuk and Qaqortoq, brightly coloured houses look like Lego blocks strewn across the hillside, set against a backdrop of snow-capped peaks and icebergs. But Greenland's top draw is its Inuit history and culture. The majority of the population today are Greenlandic Inuit; old turf huts give a sense of how their ancestors made do with very little in the harshest of conditions, while museums are packed with Norse settler artefacts.

Navigating the icebergs

GOTHENBURG

Designed by the Dutch in 1621, Gothenburg, Sweden's second city, boasts splendid Neoclassical architecture, masses of sculpture-strewn parkland and a welcoming and relaxed spirit. Cosy coffeeshops housed in traditional buildings line the pedestrianized streets of Haga, one of the oldest districts, dating back to the seventeenth century. This quaint area is known for its boutique shopping, fresh-roasted coffee and irresistibly plump, home-baked cinnamon buns.

From here, it's just a hop, skip and cycle to the newest development in the city, Jubileumsparken. This still-evolving area was the city's gift to its residents in celebration of Gothenburg's 400-year anniversary in 2021; it's home to a collection of leisure facilities including swimming pools, wooded trails and a bone-warming sauna.

In between these two areas is the heart of Gothenburg, the city centre, dotted with landscaped gardens and vast woodland parks, where restaurants and bars spill onto the wide pavements and pedestrianized squares. Rivers and canals bisect the city, ultimately leading to the Kattegat strait, home to the Gothenburg archipelago – yet another facet to this dynamic city.

Gamla Posthuset, the old post office

Haga district

Gothenburg's Botanical Garden

Mouth-watering cinnamon rolls

View over the iconic Old Man of Storr

Heading for the Black Cuillin

Tasting glasses with a variety of single-malt whiskies

Ardmore Bay on the Waternish Peninsula

Dunvegan Castle

ISLE OF SKYE

The dramatic landscapes on the Isle of Skye never seem to sit still – swerving and twisting into cliffs, plateaux, bays and peninsulas – having been squeezed into striking formations by millennia of relentless tectonics and tempestuous weather. The challenging peaks of the Cuillin Range draw in serious mountaineers, while the quirky contours of the Trotternish Peninsula offer up one photogenic panorama after another. And it pays to look out for the fossilized shoreline footprints of the dinosaurs that plodded by around 170 million years ago.

Clan castles, like Dunvegan, and decaying former crofts dot the landscape – along with traditional thatched-roof cottages – offering glimpses of a past shaped by rural Gaelic culture. Skye is high on the list of gourmets looking for world-class seafood, too – like Minch langoustine or scallops – and the air is occasionally perfumed by the roasted malts or burning peat of whisky distilleries like Talisker and Torabhaig.

ISTANBUL

Split in two by the Bosphorus, Istanbul effectively has a European and an Asian side. Yet this exotic and atmospheric city is all wonderfully Turkish, and its long and colourful history harks back to its role as the capital of the Byzantine and Ottoman empires. It's hard to know where to start, but you might want to begin by visiting the impressive Blue Mosque, Hagia Sophia, Topkapı Palace and other sites around the ancient hippodrome in Sultanahmet, and perhaps dive into the maze of the Grand Bazaar and steam-clean yourself in a hammam. Then cross the Golden Horn by tram or ferry to explore the city's modern hub that centres on Taksim Square and İstiklal Caddesi, the main pedestrian boulevard, lined with grand nineteenth-century buildings. This area has smart shopping, from local specialities to international designer outlets, interesting small *pasaj* (arcades) crammed with antiques shops to fish restaurants and rooftop eateries with sprawling, Bosphorus views.

Inside the Hagia Sophia

Grand Bazaar

Bosphorus Bridge

İstiklal Caddesi

Lake Balaton

Balaton Sound

Lake Hévíz

Windsurfing on Lake Balaton

LAKE BALATON

Lake Balaton has overflowing appeal. This freshwater landmark, the largest lake in Central Europe, sits in picturesque surrounds and brims with options for every type of traveller. Venture to the west and you'll find Lake Hévíz, the second-largest thermal lake in the world, where you can soak up the water's healing benefits; alternatively, cut through the waves as you windsurf in Szigliget or cool off in northern Balatonfelvidék while sipping on some delightfully crisp wines. Party-animals should head to the south side of the lake, with its cluster of lively resorts, or head east to Balaton Sound, the region's electronic music festival that has been running for more than ten years. Whether on the hunt for adventure, peace and quiet or energetic nightlife, Hungary's "inner sea" has got you covered.

Vines in Badacsonyi, the region on the northern shores of Lake Balaton

LES CALANQUES

Les Calanques – a series of pristine fjord-like inlets cut into the limestone cliffs that run between Marseilles and Cassis – offer excellent hiking and stunning, isolated coves. The area, which was declared a national park in 2012, protects glassy deep-blue waters, and swimming between the looming cliffs is pure heaven.

Several companies operate boat trips from the port in nearby Cassis – but if you're feeling energetic, follow the well-marked GR98 footpath from Port-Miou on the western side of town. Many people rate chic little Cassis as the best resort this side of St-Tropez; it's known for its fragrant white wine, which tantalizes the palate with hints of the herbs that cover these hills.

Calanque de Port-Miou

Notting Hill facades

LONDON

London is a thrilling place. Monuments from the city's glorious past are everywhere, from medieval banqueting halls and the great churches of Christopher Wren to eclectic Victorian architecture. You can relax in quiet Georgian squares, explore the narrow alleyways of the City of London, wander along the riverside walkways, and uncover the quirks of what is still identifiably a collection of villages. Stretching for more than 50km from east to west, London is incredibly diverse, ethnically and linguistically, offering cultural and culinary delights from right across the globe.

The UK capital's traditional sights – Big Ben, Westminster Abbey, Buckingham Palace, St Paul's Cathedral, the Tower of London and so on – continue to draw in millions of tourists every year. Things change fast though, and the regular emergence of new attractions ensures there's plenty to do. With Tate Modern and the Shard, the city boasts the world's most popular modern art museum and Western Europe's tallest building. And the city continues to grow, its cultural, nightlife and culinary scenes pushing ever onwards into neighbourhoods once well beyond the tourist radar.

Tower of London

Tate Modern

London bar

Big Ben

MAZURIAN LAKE DISTRICT

The so-called "land of a thousand lakes", Poland's Mazurian Lake District was formed more than ten thousand years ago, when retreating glaciers carved out the hollows now filled with water. A sparsely populated area of thick forests and innumerable lakes and rivers in the northeastern territory of Mazury, this is one of the country's most sought-after holiday districts, synonymous with carefree fun and relaxation. There's plenty of local colour, from sea shanties performed in Sztynort to Mrągowo's country festival and comedy nights in Lidzbark Warmiński. As you might expect, fans of water-sports will be spoilt for choice, with more than 150km of clean canals connecting hundreds of lakes. Edged by surviving tracts of unspoiled wilderness, this is perfect terrain for walking, kayaking or simply communing with nature. And if it's just some old-fashioned peace and quiet you're after, there are plenty of charming lakeside cottages where you can recharge the batteries away from big-city life.

Ełk Lake, hugged by the town of the same name

Ruins at Selinunte

Grape vines leading to the sea

The settlement of Sambuca

Local white wine

MENFI

Just a one-hour drive from Palermo Airport, Menfi's gently rolling hills ease down to white-sand beaches that fringe the enticing Mediterranean Sea. This is agricultural Italy at its best, producing sun-enriched vegetables, wine and olive oil, all available from Menfi, the town with which the area shares its name. To the west you'll find the impressive remains of Selinunte, one of the largest cities in Ancient Greece from 409 BC; in the east, there's the rambling fishing village of Sciacca, home to one of the largest fleets in Italy.

Natural beauty abounds here in Sicily – you'll see the most by exploring the area on Menfi's 90km-plus of dedicated cycle paths, the perfect way to reach the beach. In June, local wine producers throw their doors open to the public for the annual Inycon Festival, while closer to the coast, fresh seafood is served up net-to-plate at *Da Vittorio* in Porto Palo and *La Pineta* in Selinunte.

Sciacca harbour

Geirangerfjord

NORWEGIAN FJORDS

The deep gorges of the fjord landscape, with crystal-clear bright-blue waters, cascading waterfalls and endless open vistas, is enough to take the breath away of even the most jaded world traveller. Views such as that from Preikestolen (Pulpit Rock), with a sheer drop of over 600m down to the Lysefjord below, or the Lofoten Wall, as the dark, forbidding cliff wall of the Lofoten Islands is known, are sights that have converted many a visitor into a firm Norway enthusiast. The tiny hamlet of Geiranger, with only three hundred inhabitants, receives around 700,000 visitors a year, who come to enjoy the magic and splendour of narrow Geirangerfjord, without the place seeming too crowded. There is always a sense of space and room to roam in Norway.

Norway's long coastline is punctuated by more than one thousand fjords, which reach all the way from Oslo in the southeast to the Arctic north. The most dramatic are those found along the west coast, with steep mountain walls rising up from the water, and small farms clinging to every ledge and hectare of green. The fjords are beautiful, timeless and everyone's idea of the soul of Norway.

Preikestolen

Nordland fishing boat

Colourful village near Bergen

Lofoten Islands

Musée d'Orsay

Paris bistro

The Louvre

Panorama from Notre-Dame

Pompidou Centre

PARIS

Capital of romance, food, intellectuals and philosophers, famed for its historic buildings and monuments and for that indefinable *je ne sais quoi* that makes up French chic, Paris is a city that likes to live up to its myths. The very fabric of the place is exquisite, with its magnificent avenues and atmospheric little backstreets, its grand formal gardens and intimate neighbourhood squares.

The city is divided into twenty arrondissements, arranged in a spiral. Through the heart of the city flows the Seine, skirting the pair of islands where Paris was founded. The royal palace of the Louvre stands on the riverbank, along with one of the world's most distinctive landmarks – the Eiffel Tower. The Louvre is one of the world's truly outstanding museums, while the art collections of the Musée d'Orsay and Pompidou Centre are unrivalled.

Caldey Abbey

Puffins on Skomer Island

Pembrokeshire Coast National Park Trail

Pentre Ifan dolmen

PEMBROKESHIRE

Surrounded by the Atlantic on three sides, and nestled in Wales' most south-westerly corner, picturesque Pembrokeshire is a place of wild wonder, ancient history and contemporary vitality.

Pembrokeshire's beaches are truly topnotch, from Caribbean-esque Barafundle Bay to the sand dune-backed surfing hotspot of Freshwater East. Then there's the internationally renowned Pembrokeshire Coast National Park Trail that undulates through spectacular scenery and offers walkers sightings of seals and dolphins, as well as stunning geological formations such as Stack Rocks.

Pembrokeshire's coastline is dappled with distinctive islands, among them Skomer, which is home to half the world's population of Manx shearwaters, and the nesting sites of tens of thousands of puffins. Accessed from the vibrant harbour town of Tenby, culturally unique Caldey Island is home to a Cistercian monk community whose recorded history stretches back 1500 years. The county is also rich in castles and prehistoric sites, among them the mighty Pentre Ifan dolmen.

Barafundle Bay

Street and houses in the Kapana district

Remains of the ancient Roman stadium in Plovdiv's centre

Plovdiv's Roman amphitheatre

Dzhumaya Mosque

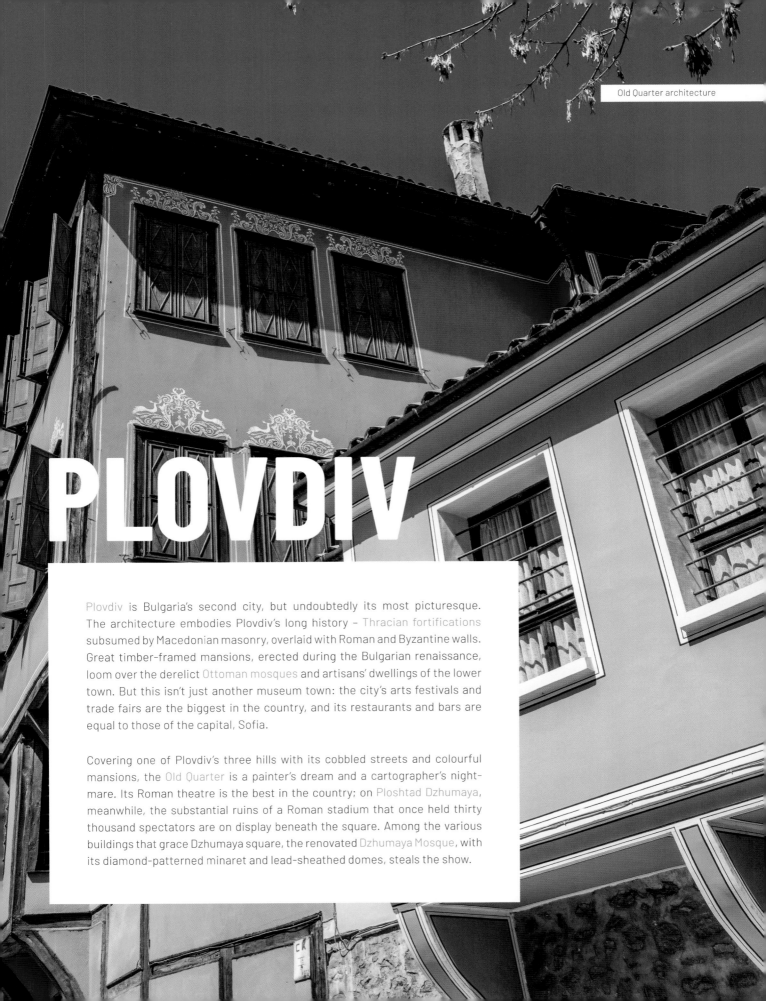

PLOVDIV

Plovdiv is Bulgaria's second city, but undoubtedly its most picturesque. The architecture embodies Plovdiv's long history – Thracian fortifications subsumed by Macedonian masonry, overlaid with Roman and Byzantine walls. Great timber-framed mansions, erected during the Bulgarian renaissance, loom over the derelict Ottoman mosques and artisans' dwellings of the lower town. But this isn't just another museum town: the city's arts festivals and trade fairs are the biggest in the country, and its restaurants and bars are equal to those of the capital, Sofia.

Covering one of Plovdiv's three hills with its cobbled streets and colourful mansions, the Old Quarter is a painter's dream and a cartographer's nightmare. Its Roman theatre is the best in the country; on Ploshtad Dzhumaya, meanwhile, the substantial ruins of a Roman stadium that once held thirty thousand spectators are on display beneath the square. Among the various buildings that grace Dzhumaya square, the renovated Dzhumaya Mosque, with its diamond-patterned minaret and lead-sheathed domes, steals the show.

PORTO

Hugging the steep northern banks of the Rio Douro, Porto is irresistibly pictur-esque. Pastel-fronted townhouses wind up the hilltop from the UNESCO-inscribed Ribeira, where eateries serve fresh sardines and seafood galore. As you climb up the shelving riverbank, the views across to Vila Nova de Gaia on the opposite bank become increasingly spectacular. It is in Gaia, on the south side of the river, that you'll find the city's world-famous port lodges – Porto having given the fortified wine its name. Graham's, Taylor's and Churchill's are ones to watch. Alternatively, for a Portuguese-run outfit, pay a visit to Ferreira, which was founded more than 250 years ago in an old convent. Anyone after an authentic foodie experience, meanwhile, will want to try the francesinha. This gut-busting sandwich is a love-it-or-hate-it gig, with bread, pork, sausage and steak, doused in a thick tomato and beer sauce and melted cheese, and finished with a fried egg on top.

Elsewhere, there are plenty of architectural and cultural gems to explore, from the Nasoni-designed Torre dos Clérigos to the striking cathedral. You only have to wander the streets to stumble across beautiful facades clad in iconic blue-and-white *azulejos* (tiles); the Estação de São Bento, the city's central station, and the Igreja de São Ildefonso, are two of the most impressive examples. Contemporary-art lovers should head for Serralves to muse on its world-class collection and the Serralves Villa, an enchanting pink Art Deco building constructed in the 1930s.

Serralves Villa

PRAGUE

Few other European capitals look quite as beautiful as Prague, with some six hundred years of architecture virtually untouched by natural disaster or war. Straddling the winding River Vltava, with a steep wooded hill to one side, the city retains much of its medieval layout, and its rich mantle of Baroque, Rococo and Art Nouveau buildings have successfully escaped the vanities and excesses of modern development.

Prague is divided into two unequal halves by the river, which meanders through the heart of the Czech capital and features one of its most enduring landmarks, Charles Bridge. Built during the city's medieval golden age, this stone bridge, with its parade of Baroque statuary, still forms the chief link between the more central old town, or Staré Město, on the right bank, and Prague's hilltop castle on the left.

The castle is a vast complex, which towers over the rest of the city and supplies the classic picture-postcard image of Prague. Spread across the slopes below are the wonderful cobbled streets and secret walled gardens of Malá Strana, little changed in the two hundred years since Mozart walked them.

Charles Bridge

Church of Our Lady before Týn

Wolfgang Amadeus Mozart waxwork at the Grévin Prague

Prague's bridges

The Pantheon at night

Temple of Saturn, Roman Forum

Spiral staircase in the Vatican Museums

Trevi Fountain

ROME

Dubbed the Eternal City by poets and artists, Rome inspires the mind, appeals to the senses and captures the heart. Its eras crowd in on top of one another to a remarkable degree: there are medieval churches atop ancient basilicas and palaces, houses and apartment blocks that incorporate fragments of Roman columns and inscriptions, and roads and piazzas that follow the lines of ancient amphitheatres and stadiums.

Rome is an immense outdoor museum, and it's not an easy place to absorb on one visit. The city packs in a staggering number of iconic sights: the Colosseum, the most recognizable and perhaps the greatest ancient Roman monument of them all; the Roman Forum, the majestic ruins of the civic centre of Ancient Rome; Trevi Fountain; Piazza di Spagna, with the Spanish Steps and Keats-Shelley House; the Pantheon, Rome's most intact ancient sight; and the Vatican Museums – meriting a lifetime's study in their own right but most famed for Michelangelo's breathtaking ceiling in the Sistine Chapel.

Part of Rome's allure is stumbling across things by accident and gradually piecing the city together – just remember to pause at the superb pizzerias and *gelaterie* along the way.

Sagrada Família facade

Exterior statues

Intricate relief carving

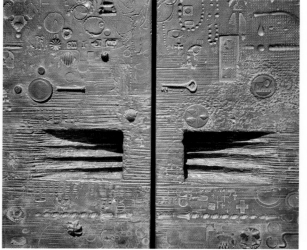

Religious door inscription

SAGRADA FAMÍLIA

Antoni Gaudí's unfinished masterpiece is one of Spain's truly essential sights. As work on the Basilica de la Sagrada Família races towards completion, and its extraordinary towers climb ever closer towards the heavens, the glorious, overpowering church of the "Sacred Family" is now more than ever a symbol for Barcelona, and even the coldest hearts will find it inspirational in both form and spirit.

Though work began in 1882 by public subscription, Antoni Gaudí took over on the Sagrada Família two years later. When he died – after being hit by a tram – in 1926, all Barcelona turned out for his funeral procession, after which Gaudí was buried in the Sagrada Família crypt. Only one facade of the church was then complete. Work stalled during the Civil War, with most of Gaudí's original plans and models lost in the turmoil. Construction finally restarted, amid great controversy, in the 1950s.

Even if the builders fail to meet their current target of finishing the church to mark the centenary of Gaudí's death in 2026, it looks like the Sagrada Família will finally be completed within the next decade.

Ceiling detail

Peterhof

Bank Bridge lions

The Church of the Saviour on the Spilled Blood

The Winter Palace

ST PETERSBURG

Russia's most beautiful city was founded by Peter the Great in 1702 on the marshy banks of the Neva River. Built on 44 islands set among canals and rivers and traversed by more than four hundred bridges, St Petersburg is a city where pastel-coloured palaces are reflected in the canals, where mansions and churches harmoniously surround every square, and where statues stand in silent watch over gardens and parks.

St Petersburg is one of the world's greatest cities for art-lovers, too, filled with the glories of pre-revolutionary architecture and the best art collections in Russia. The Hermitage, housed in the Winter Palace, is one of the world's largest and most dazzling museums, while just behind it and rich in history, Palace Square has witnessed murder, conspiracy and the coup that ousted the tsar. If you tire of urban beauty, you can go out to the ring of palace estates that encircle the city. Whatever your fancy, after a few days in St Petersburg, few fail to fall under the city's spell.

Palace Square

TUSCANY

The Renaissance, that frenzy of curiosity and creativity that unleashed the modern world, was born in Florence, a legendary city still overflowing with fine art and architecture. Almost as exquisite are Siena, built around a stunning cathedral, walled Lucca and Pisa, with its famous leaning tower. Between these places, the unchanging countryside of Tuscany is any artist's dream, its white roads – lined with brushstroke cypress trees – threading their way through emerald-green vineyards and golden fields of wheat. You will soon lose count of the fortified hilltop villages filled with stone mansions and surmounted by elegant towers. Each long view and every detail is a delight; the food and wine a real pleasure. Where else could Michelangelo and Leonardo da Vinci have been born?

The world-famous Leaning Tower of Pisa

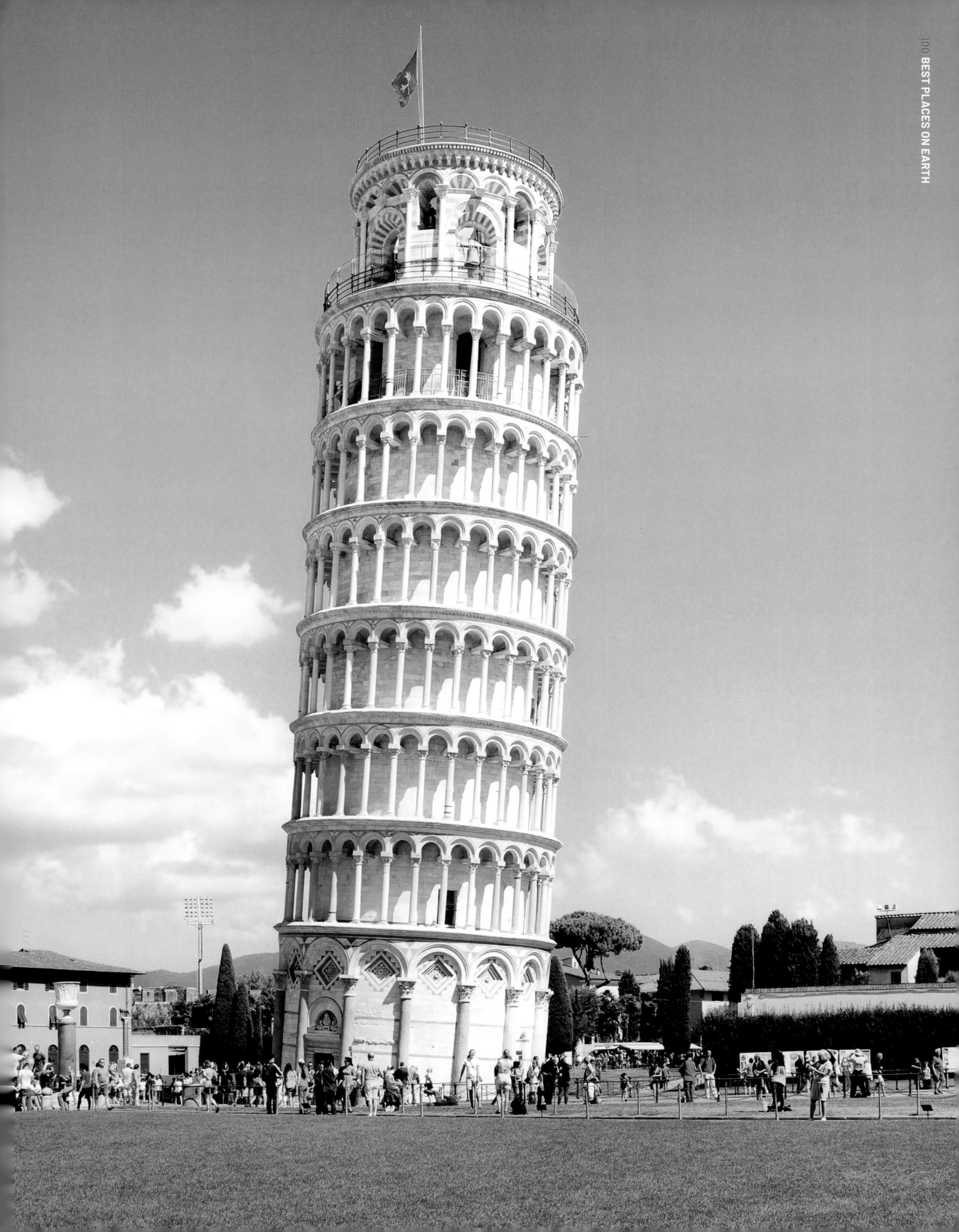

Hall of Mirrors

Gardens of Versailles

Inside the Grand Trianon château

Ceiling painting in Salon d'Hercule

Latona Fountain

VERSAILLES

The Sun King of France did nothing by halves. Driven by envy of his finance minister's château at Vaux-le-Vicomte, the young Louis XIV recruited the same design team – architect Le Vau, painter Le Brun and gardener Le Nôtre – to create a palace a hundred times bigger. The result, Versailles, is the palace against which all other palaces are judged. The building, with its endless gilded chambers, speaks of unlimited royal power, while its landscaped grounds epitomize the Enlightenment attitude that human beings have been put on earth to subdue nature.

In its heyday, Versailles was the headquarters of every arm of state, a community of twenty thousand people from statesmen and sycophants to stable boys. It is now one of the biggest attractions in France, but it's at its very best on Saturday nights in summer, when the monumental fountains are floodlit and set to Baroque music.

USA,
MEXICO &
CANADA

Palm Springs
CALIFORNIA
California
5XRY616
California
4VRT113

CAMPECHE

The historic centre of Campeche is a strong contender for Mexico's prettiest settlement. Endorsed by UNESCO, its tightly gridded streets are lined by pastel-coloured buildings with gleaming white doorways. But the area has much more to offer than appealing aesthetics. Campeche's robust city walls have been solidly rebuilt, and their intermittent bulwarks hold a collection of history and culture museums showcasing some of the finest Maya artefacts in the region.

Elsewhere, the palm-lined malecón provides stunning sunset views out over the Gulf of Mexico; its cannon-topped fortresses evoke a time when city defences were needed to repel swashbuckling European pirates. In the evening, the focal point becomes leafy Parque Principal – overlooked by the twin-towered cathedral – where weekly light shows depict the region's history, from the asteroid that crashed into Earth nearby, wiping out the dinosaurs, through to the present day.

A line up of colourful Campeche houses

A canon on the malecón

The Land Gate

Campeche's cathedral

Canoeing on Lake Louise in Banff National Park

Jasper National Park resident

Canoes docked at Lake Moraine in Banff National Park

Icefields Parkway

A hiker contemplates Columbia Icefield and Athabasca Glacier

CANADIAN ROCKIES

While its jagged peaks have graced many a screensaver, nothing can prepare you for the raw beauty of the Canadian Rockies. As the Canadian segment of the North American Rocky Mountains, this area – weaving through the provinces of Alberta and British Columbia – is home to a tremendous landscape of mountains and lakes, and one of the most dramatic road trips in the world: the Icefields Parkway.

The region is celebrated for its outdoor activities, blow-you-away views and diverse wildlife. Black and brown bears cause frequent traffic jams, canoeing on turquoise lakes makes for a serene pastime and impressive sights are easily accessible, from Athabasca Glacier to Johnston Canyon. While popular bases Lake Louise and Banff are certainly worth a visit, the real draw of the Canadian Rockies is in quiet contemplation on its lonely hiking trails, enveloped by the scent of pine. So lace up your walking boots and breathe in the region's awesome natural architecture.

Downtown Cleveland seen from the harbour

Cleveland residential street

Exhibit at the Cleveland Museum of Art

West Side Market

CLEVELAND

Perched on the shoreline of Lake Erie in northeastern Ohio, Cleveland is part of the expansive Great Lakes region. Victorian clapboard houses line the leafy streets with the unhurriedness of small-town charm, but the city roars into action with a buzzing music scene – with the likes of the legendary Rock 'n' Roll Hall of Fame and the renowned Cleveland Orchestra – as well as homegrown chefs and their award-winning restaurants. There are plenty of heavyweight cultural attractions, too. Picks of the bunch include the Cleveland History Center, complete with an expansive automobile collection (a nod to the city's once-premier industry); the superlative Museum of Art, displaying more than 45,000 ancient and modern works of art; and the vibrant West Side Market, where nineteenth-century immigrants once shopped for their native foods. Whether you're an art-lover, food-fanatic or you simply want to soak up the highlights, Cleveland can't be beat.

Maroon Lake

Mural at Denver Central Market

Red Rocks amphitheatre

Trail Ridge Road sunset

DENVER AND COLORADO

It's impossible not to have a good time in Colorado. Whether you're biking between brewpubs on Breckenridge's craft-beer trail, hiking in the wilderness, exploring ancient Native American cliff dwellings or driving across the Continental Divide along the Trail Ridge Road – the highest paved road on the continent – you're surrounded by gorgeous Rocky Mountain scenery.

For more urban pleasures, the nightlife in Denver is second to none, with dozens of great bars and restaurants oozing laidback, Colorado cool. Its lively arts scene, from the architecturally stunning Denver Art Museum to the vivid street murals of the RiNo district, takes a leap into the cutting edge in 2021 with the opening of Meow Wolf, a mind-blowing immersive art installation. Leave the city buzz behind and head to Red Rocks, the world's finest open-air amphitheatre, for a concert under the stars or a morning yoga session, then venture on into Colorado's glorious mountains.

Denver Art Museum

GRAND CANYON

Although almost five million people visit Grand Canyon National Park every year, the canyon itself remains beyond the grasp of human imagination. No photograph, no statistics, can prepare you for such immensity. Billions of years of the earth's geologic history is frozen in bright bands of pink, beige, orange, rust and gold on the canyon walls. Peer into the abyss to glimpse a sliver of the Colorado River, nearly 2km below, which carved out the canyon some six billion years ago. By contrast, the national park – a UNESCO World Heritage Site – has only just past the century mark.

Spend at least a full day here, watching the colours change in the shifting light. The vast majority of visitors come to the South Rim and linger at the viewpoints, spotting rare California condors soaring on the breeze, though the North Rim can be a lot more evocative by virtue of its isolation. Wherever you go, you are gazing at one of the Seven Wonders of the Natural World. Breathe it in.

A Grand Canyon sunrise

Kīlauea erupting

HAWAI'I VOLCANOES NATIONAL PARK

A sweet smell lingers in the air at Hawai'i Volcanoes National Park, no matter the time of year. Its harbingers are the wildflowers that carpet the park's fertile lava fields, masking the faintly sulphuric tangs and bringing colour to this dark, lunar landscape. Jungles also abound, surrounding the crater rim of vast Kīlauea, one of the world's largest volcanoes, threatening to wipe out the vegetation with a fresh flow of molten lava. Steam vents interrupt the terrain: deep holes where vivid green epiphytes grow in the cracks of the jagged brown rock and vapour escapes the earth. In this land of steam and fire, visitors can walk across an active lava field, see the glow of molten rock as it rises and bubbles from the volcanoes, and drive along Chain of Craters Road all the way to the coast, where the lava has been stopped in its tracks and turned to black rock.

Pu'u Loa petroglyphs, carved into hardened lava

Lava tube

Jungle trail

Molten lava flowing into the Pacific Ocean on Big Island

MONUMENT VALLEY

From Stagecoach to Buster Scruggs, Monument Valley has been immortalized on the silver screen from the earliest days of Hollywood cinema. This tract of rugged wilderness epitomizes both the Wild West's endless allure and its mortal fragility, but these huge sandstone buttes, rising up from the arid red desert, are actually the product of millions of years of climatic attrition.

Long before any European set eyes on – or gave the current name to – Monument Valley, the natural wonders were already considered sacred by the Navajo Nation, and are now encompassed by their wider ancestral lands.

This whole region is best experienced by driving along the open road. Better yet, access restricted areas by joining a guided horseback tour, travelling through the canyons the traditional way. Nearby, amid other geological marvels – natural stone arches and the like – is the occasional prehistoric cave dwelling, proof that this seemingly inhospitable region has enchanted humans for millennia.

View from Hunts Mesa

Mural on Lower East Side

Rockefeller Center

Wall Street

Times Square

NEW YORK CITY

Cultural and financial capital of the USA, if not the world, New York City is an adrenaline-charged, history-laden place that holds immense romantic appeal for visitors. Its past is visible in the tangled lanes of Wall Street and tenements of the Lower East Side; meanwhile, towering skyscrapers serve as monuments of the modern age. Street life buzzes round the clock and shifts markedly from one area to the next. The waterfront, redeveloped in many places, and the landscaped green spaces – notably Central Park – give the city a chance to catch its breath. Iconic cultural symbols – the neon of Times Square, the sculptures at Rockefeller Center – always seem just a stone's throw away. For raw energy, dynamism and social diversity, you'd be hard-pressed to top it; simply put, there's no place quite like it.

Central Park

Mid-century architecture

Glitz and glamour at Palm Springs Pride

Life is lived outside in Palm Springs

Mount San Jacinto State Park

PALM SPRINGS

Popularized in the 1950s by studio-owned movie stars whose contracts kept them within two hours of Hollywood, showbiz glamour still flows effortlessly around the delightful small city of Palm Springs. Progressive architects and forward-thinking designers created cutting-edge modernist homes and offices, leaving a unique collection of dynamic mid-twentieth century buildings. The climate is perfect for outdoor living almost year-round, with open-air concerts, alfresco dining, cycling, trail hiking and almost every recreation activity ever invented. Glimpses of snow-covered mountains, framed by clear blue skies, are visible through the palm trees on a winter's day. Mount San Jacinto State Park can be reached by cable car, giving stunning views along the entire Coachella Valley. Across the valley, meanwhile, is Joshua Tree National Park, a vast protected area of pristine desert, weathered granite rock formations and abandoned gold mines. The area's pioneering spirit continues today – pretty much anything goes in this laid-back LGBTQ-friendly Californian hotspot.

TEOTIHUACAN

Once the largest city in the Americas – with a burgeoning collection of flourishing temples, palaces and pyramids dedicated to celestial bodies like the sun and the moon – Teotihuacan has never lost its ability to inspire awe. Arranged around the broad, 2.5km-long Avenue of the Dead, this vast settlement served as a religious ceremonial centre, although its origins remain uncertain.

Teotihuacan was suddenly abandoned in the seventh century and never reoccupied – why, nobody knows – but its sturdy structures endure. It's easy here, stood atop the 64-metre-tall Pirámide del Sol, to picture holy men of old making blood sacrifices to appease deities like the rain-god Tlaloc.

Murals and relief carvings still adorn the walls of several palaces and temples, like those of plumed serpents and big cats inside the palaces of the Quetzal Butterfly or the Jaguars. The resident museum showcases treasures found on archeological digs around the site – gold jewellery, stone carvings and intact murals – and you'll want to spend an entire day here to drink it all in.

Pyrámide del Sol

Replica of Teotihuacan Temple at the National Museum of Anthropology, Mexico City

Avenue of the Dead

Tlaloc vessel

Steller sea lion

Lumber factory near Telegraph Cove

Parliament Buildings, Victoria

Killer whale

VANCOUVER AND AROUND

The gateway to Canada's western wilderness is hip and vibrant Vancouver. The city's boutique shops are stocked with local labels, its fine-dining restaurants serve fresher-than-fresh seafood and its food trucks dole out inventive dishes from around the world. Its varied nightlife scene heralds some fabulous signature cocktails, tomorrow's hangover taken care of by the city's coffee-shop movement, which ensures top-quality roasts.

Be sure to venture beyond the city borders, too. A rugged sliver of land cast adrift from mainland Canada, Vancouver Island may only be a ninety-minute boat journey from Vancouver, but it feels worlds apart. Its waters teem with whales, otters and dolphins, while bears and wolves roam inland. There is more to this island than wildlife, though. Cowichan Valley's patchwork of vineyards is an epicurean enclave, with wine tours and farm-to-table dining galore.

Whistler Blackcomb is also within easy reach of Vancouver, with bears, cougars and deer among the bigger species roving its snowy peaks, and salmon swelling the rivers. Consistently cited as one of the best places to ski in the world, it offers the same of mountain biking and wooded hikes in the summer months.

Red country barn

Skiing in Stowe

Vermont welcome sign

Maple syrup

Autumn colours in Vermont

VERMONT

With its white churches and barns, covered bridges and clapboard houses, snowy woods and maple syrup, Vermont comes closer than any other New England state to fulfilling the quintessential image of small-town Yankee America. Much of the state is smothered by verdant, mountainous forests and valleys painted in a thousand shades of green; the name Vermont supposedly comes from the French *vert mont,* or green mountain.

Tourism here is largely activity-oriented, and though the state's rural charms can be enjoyed year-round, most visitors come during two well-defined seasons: to see the spectacular fall foliage in the first two weeks of October – when the green leaves of summer turn to vivid oranges, yellows and reds – and to ski in the depths of winter, when resorts such as Killington and Stowe spring to life. Vermont's fresh air and gorgeous scenery will make the soul sing.

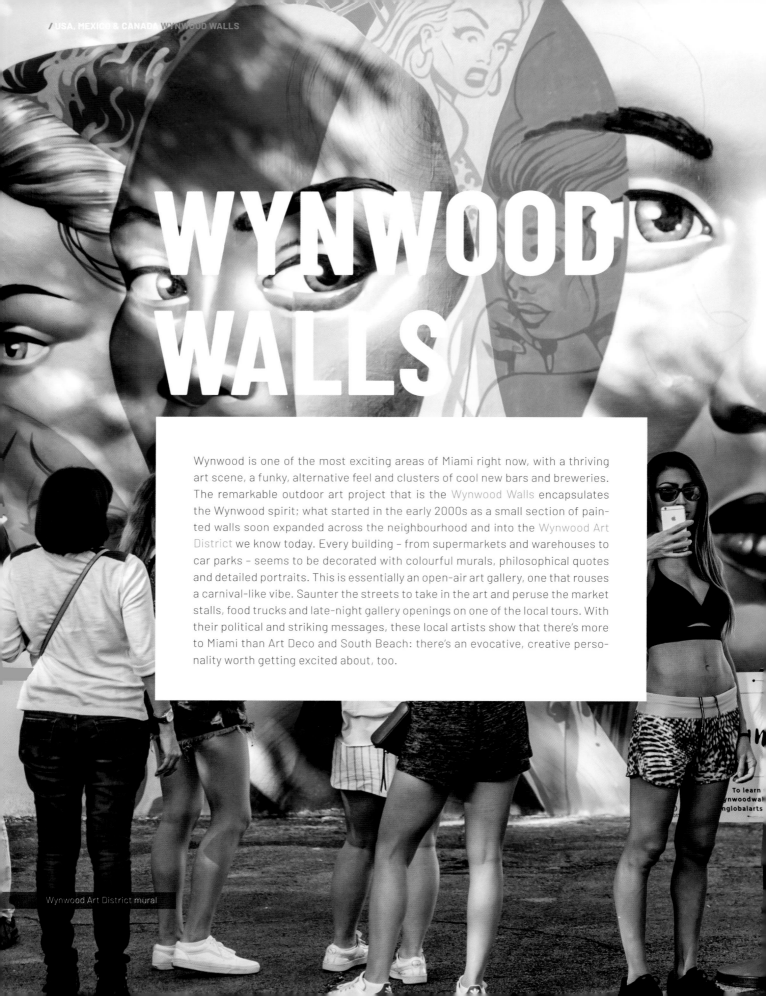

WYNWOOD WALLS

Wynwood is one of the most exciting areas of Miami right now, with a thriving art scene, a funky, alternative feel and clusters of cool new bars and breweries. The remarkable outdoor art project that is the Wynwood Walls encapsulates the Wynwood spirit; what started in the early 2000s as a small section of painted walls soon expanded across the neighbourhood and into the Wynwood Art District we know today. Every building – from supermarkets and warehouses to car parks – seems to be decorated with colourful murals, philosophical quotes and detailed portraits. This is essentially an open-air art gallery, one that rouses a carnival-like vibe. Saunter the streets to take in the art and peruse the market stalls, food trucks and late-night gallery openings on one of the local tours. With their political and striking messages, these local artists show that there's more to Miami than Art Deco and South Beach: there's an evocative, creative personality worth getting excited about, too.

Wynwood Art District mural

Herd of bison in Hayden Valley

YELLOWSTONE NATIONAL PARK

America's oldest and easily its most famous national park, Yellowstone draws in the punters for good reason: the sheer diversity of what's on offer is mind-bending. Not only does Yellowstone deliver jaw-dropping mountain scenery, from the scintillating colours of the Grand Canyon of the Yellowstone to the deep-azure Yellowstone Lake and wild flower-filled meadows, but it's jam-packed with so much wildlife you might think you've arrived at a safari park. Shambling grizzly bears, vast herds of heavy-bearded bison (buffalo) and horned elk mingle with marmots, prairie dogs, eagles, coyotes and more than a dozen elusive wolf packs on the prowl.

What really sets Yellowstone apart, however, is that this is one of the world's largest volcanoes, with thermal activity providing half the world's geysers, thousands of fumaroles jetting plumes of steam, mud pots gurgling with acid-dissolved muds and clays, and, of course, hot springs. The park might not look like a volcano, but that's because the caldera is so big – 55km by 72km – and because, thankfully, it hasn't exploded for 640,000 years.

Yellowstone Lake

Great Fountain Geyser

Grizzly bear

Majestic bull elk

CENTRAL AMERICA, SOUTH AMERICA & THE CARIBBEAN

Guide in the Parque Nacional Madidi

The Beni River, Parque Nacional Madidi

Jesuit Mission church in San José de Chiquitos

Caymen line a riverbank

Jaguar in Madidi

BOLIVIAN AMAZON AND CHIQUITOS

The Bolivian Amazon and Chiquitos regions are incredible places to explore. In the west, Parque Nacional Madidi covers nearly 20,000 square kilometres of the upper Amazon River basin. This bewitching national park enjoys the distinction of being the most biodiverse protected area on earth, home to literally thousands of species, notably anacondas, jaguars and pink dolphins. Over in the east, meanwhile, the city of Trinidad is the jumping-off point for epic boat trips in search of a mysterious collection of ancient earthworks that helped inspire the myth of El Dorado. Further south, Chiquitos boasts a remarkable collection of seventeenth- and eighteenth-century Jesuit churches, many of them UNESCO World Heritage sites.

Rampant wildfires in 2019 in the Brazilian Amazon drew global attention, yet there was little coverage of similarly devastating blazes in neighbouring Bolivia. By supporting the many eco-tourism projects in the Bolivian Amazon and Chiquitos regions – which include rainforest lodges owned by indigenous communities, conservation-focused tour companies and privately run wildlife reserves, as well as national parks – travellers can help locals to rebuild their lives and prevent future environmental catastrophes.

BUENOS AIRES

Of all South America's capitals, Buenos Aires has the most going for it. Seductive and cultured, sophisticated yet earthy, eclectic but with a strong identity, it never bores, seldom sleeps and invariably mesmerizes its visitors. Influenced by the great European cities, Buenos Aires nonetheless has its own distinct personality, enhanced by proud traditions, including football, tango and *mate*. On one flank lap the caramel-hued waters of the Río de Plata, the world's widest estuary: signs of the city's regained prosperity include wharves stacked high with containers and the busy ship terminus. To the west and south, the verdant Pampas – historically the source of the city's food and wealth – meld seamlessly into its vast suburbs.

Modern Buenos Aires enjoys an incomparable lifestyle. Elegant restaurants, glamourous bars, historic cafés and heaving nightclubs, plus a world-class opera house, countless theatres, avant-garde galleries and French-style palaces all underscore its attachment to the arts and its eternal sense of style. Another boon is the abundance of parks and gardens, plus the many trees lining the streets and providing shade in the lively plazas that dot the huge metropolis; they add welcome splashes of colour, particularly when ablaze with yellow, pink and mauve blooms in spring and autumn.

Colourful La Boca district

Hiking in the Fuegian Andes

Cape Horn scenery

Guanaco, a close relation of the llama

Puerto Montt

CHILEAN PATAGONIA AND TIERRA DEL FUEGO

Southern Chile encompasses some of the most dramatic landscapes in South America: snow-covered Andean peaks, simmering volcanoes, vast ice fields, gold-hued steppe, deep fjords and dense sub-polar forests.

Thanks to an ambitious sustainable-tourism project, there is a renewed focus on the sparsely populated region of Patagonia and Tierra del Fuego. Launched in 2018 following a huge donation of private land to the Chilean state, the Ruta de los Parques (Route of Parks) is now starting to take shape. Extending 2736km from the city of Puerto Montt to Cape Horn, the most southerly tip of the continent, it links up seventeen national parks with the aim of conserving fragile ecosystems and providing economic opportunities for isolated communities.

Patagonia was christened by Portuguese explorer Ferdinand Magellan who, on making landfall at San Julián (in modern-day Argentina) in 1520, thought the tall Tehuelche natives had unusually big feet – "pata" is Spanish for "foot". Still wild and wondrous, this is one of the world's most majestic, empty and awe-inspiring regions.

A brown-throated sloth

COSTA RICA

With its inspiring *pura-vida* (pure-life) ethos and commitment to becoming carbon neutral in 2021, army-less Costa Rica is the ultimate destination for adventurous nature-lovers and environmentally minded travellers.

Despite only taking up 0.03 percent of the planet, Costa Rica contains a staggering five percent of the world's biodiversity, with 52 hummingbird species (making it the hummingbird capital of the world) and more than nine hundred bird species in total, including the aptly named resplendent quetzal. Costa Rica's mammalian diversity is exceptional too, with national parks protecting the habitats of everything from sloths, anteaters and armadillos to peccaries, tapiers and howler monkeys, and elusive ocelots, pumas and jaguars.

Adventurers will love zip-lining the Monteverde Cloud Forest, surfing the Pacific Coast and hiking the awe-inspiring Arenal Volcano National Park, while culture-vultures will adore the country's ancient archeological sites, among them Turrialba's Guayabo National Monument, the largest pre-Columbian ruins discovered in Costa Rica to date.

DOMINICA

Visit Dominica once and you'll yearn to return. Landing on this dramatic island in the Lesser Antilles feels like descending into an untouched jungle, and though there are plenty of classic Caribbean coves, it's the green, virgin landscapes that tug at the heartstrings. Born of volcanoes, Dominica is best characterized by its majestic mountains, verdant rainforests, rushing rivers and wild waterfalls.

Fittingly nicknamed the Nature Island, Dominica has the world's highest concentration of live volcanoes, and its Boiling Lake is the second largest of its kind on earth. With outstanding diving sites, Dominica is the only place sperm whales are sighted year-round. Back on land, the Waitukubuli Trail is a nature-lover's delight, affording opportunities to spot endemic sisserou and jaco parrots.

Alongside Dominica's natural bounty, the island is home to the world's last community of Kalinago, a people who journeyed from the Orinoco Delta some six-hundred years ago and gave Dominica its pre-Columbian name, Waitukubuli ("tall is her body").

Emerald Pool waterfall

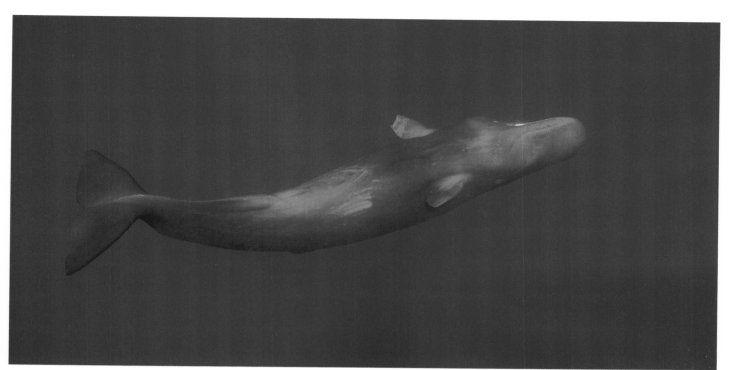

Swimming with sperm whales

Wavine Cyrique waterfall and beach

Waitukubuli National Trail sign

EASTER ISLAND

Few places have a culture quite as enigmatic as Easter Island. Despite measuring just 22 kilometres in length, it's an open-air museum on a mammoth scale. The star attractions are the 887 mysterious, monolithic *moai* statues that dot the coastline, some erected on ceremonial platforms, others abandoned in the grass. All were carved centuries ago from soft, volcanic tuff to represent and honour now long-dead ancestors.

Elsewhere, the islanders' Rapanui culture is emphatically alive. February brings the two-week smorgasbord of high-adrenaline – and perilous – events show-casing the islanders' exceptional physical prowess. During the rest of the year, watch heavily tattooed dance troupes stamping to the beat of Polynesian music in Hanga Roa's nightly performances.

Beyond the town, it's all about nature, with the peak of Volcán Terevaka granting extraordinary views of the foaming, wild ocean beyond the island's shores, while further north, tourists can linger on palm-studded, white-sand beaches.

Ahu Tongariki - the largest *ahu* on the island

View from Bartolomé Island

GALÁPAGOS ISLANDS

It's quite humbling that thirteen scarred volcanic islands and more than a hundred islets, scattered across 45,000 square kilometres of ocean, 960km adrift from the Ecuadorian mainland, should have been so instrumental in changing humanity's perception of itself. Yet it was the forbidding Galápagos Islands – known for their diverse range of species – that allowed Darwin to formulate his theory of evolution, catapulting science into the modern era. The main island, Santa Cruz, holds the Charles Darwin Research Station, where visitors can learn more about his research.

Today the archipelago's matchless wildlife, stunning scenery and unique history make it the world's premier wildlife destination. The animals that have carved out an existence on these islands have a legendary fearlessness which results in close-up encounters that are impossible anywhere else on earth. Seals sleep onshore and play in the shallow water of the harbours, giant tortoises amble along unfinished roads and marine iguanas bask in the sun on black volcanic rocks before launching themselves into the crashing waves. The waters are filled with reef sharks, turtles and swarms of reef fish, while whale sharks, hammerheads, manta rays, whales and dolphins can be spotted offshore.

Marine iguana

Resident dolphin

Charles Darwin Research Station, Santa Cruz

Giant tortoise

Guayaquil skyline at sunset, seen from Las Peñas

Colourful buildings in Las Penas

Malecón 2000

Church in Guayaquil

LAS PEÑAS

Stunning views over the city of Guayaquil from Las Peñas more than compensate for the 444 steps you'll have to climb to get here. This quaint hillside neighbourhood was the first area settled in Guayaquil, Ecuador and dates back more than four hundred years. Since it was first inhabited, the district has been rebuilt many times over, mainly as a result of fire damage. The stepped route to the pinnacle takes in cobbled streets, passing layers of brightly painted restaurants, shops and bars on its way. The small Iglesia del Cerro Santa Ana sits at the top, where views across the sprawling city, the river Guayas and the Malecón 2000 will take your breath away. To see Guayaquil at its best, ascend just before the sun sets behind the colourful houses on the western side of Las Peñas, when day turns to dusk and the first streetlights begin to flicker.

Piled houses in Las Peñas

MACHU PICCHU

As the sun climbs above the serrated ridges of the surrounding mountains and carves its way between geometric stone plazas and palaces, you're struck by the very same magic that has enthralled visitors since this citadel was "rediscovered" in 1911. Offering one of the most substantial legacies of the Inca civilization, Machu Picchu grants unparalleled access to an empire that once stretched for 4000km.

But part of what makes this archeological site so tantalizing is the experience of getting there. For many, it's on foot along the paved, former Inca road known as the Inca Trail, or the higher-still Salkantay, which climbs giddy 4600m passes.

As tourist numbers continue to increase, those wanting to avoid the crowds should head instead to the archeological complex of Kuélap. Situated in northern Peru, 420 circular stone dwellings top a vertiginous mountain plateau and are some thousand years older than the youthful Machu Picchu.

Llama in front of Machu Picchu

NAZCA LINES

One of the great mysteries of South America, the Nazca Lines are a series of animal figures and geometric shapes, none of them repeated and some up to 200m in length, drawn across some 500 square kilometres of the bleak, stony Pampa de San José in Peru. Each one, even such complicated motifs as a spider monkey and hummingbird, is executed in a single continuous line, most created by clearing away the brush and hard stones of the plain to reveal the fine dust beneath. Theories abound as to what their purpose was – from landing strips for alien spaceships to some kind of agricultural calendar, aligned with constellations above, to help regulate the planting and harvesting of crops. More recent satellite imaging suggests the lines were connected to a sophisticated ancient aqueduct system. Regardless of why they were made, the Lines are among the strangest and most unforgettable sights in South America.

The Spiral

The Hummingbird

The Spider Monkey

The Spaceman

Basílica de la Asunción, León

Corn Island beach

Granada shop

Cerro Negro crater

NICARAGUA

While tourism booms in nearby Costa Rica and Belize, Nicaragua has remained largely under the radar. Yet this beautiful and friendly country has all the charms of its Central American neighbours – and more. It counts the second-largest rainforest in the Americas (after the Amazon) among its 78 wildlife refuges and biosphere reserves, which harbour exotic animals and brightly coloured macaws, toucans and other birds. Lovely Pacific beaches boast prime surfing spots, while the white Caribbean sands of the Corn Islands are a diving and snorkelling paradise.

Nicaragua is a land of lakes and volcanoes, with stunning landscapes everywhere you go. You can hike the volcanoes, and sandboard down lava-covered slopes at Cerro Negro. Be sure to explore the old colonial cities, too: charming Granada, with its cobbled streets and brightly painted houses, and earthy León with its magnificent cathedral and political murals.

RIO DE JANEIRO

The citizens of the thirteen-million-strong city of Rio de Janeiro call it the Cidade Marvilhosa – and there can't be much argument about that. Although riven by inequality, Rio has style. Its international renown is bolstered by some of the greatest landmarks in the world: the Corcovado mountain supporting the great statue of Christ the Redeemer; the rounded incline of Sugar Loaf mountain, standing at the entrance to the bay; and the famous sweeps of Copacabana and Ipanema beaches, probably the most notable lengths of sands on the planet. It's a setting enhanced annually by the frenetic sensuality of Carnaval, an explosive celebration that – for many people – sums up Rio and its citizens, the *cariocas*.

The Selarón Steps

Locals playing on Ipanema

Copacabana

Christ the Redeemer

Carnaval dancer

SANTIAGO DE CUBA

From its perch at the eastern reaches of the forest-clad Sierra Maestra, Cuba's largest mountain range, Santiago de Cuba serenades its guests with the sweet sounds of tres guitars, maracas, bongos and tropical voices from moody little hideouts all over the city. The country's second city is, musically speaking, its first, the birthplace of almost all the traditional styles that have made the country a global musical phenomenon. Enjoying a renaissance set in motion by its 500th anniversary in 2015, the bustling centre is brimming with brilliantly renovated neo-colonial hotels, many of them dotted along the newly pedestrianized, pulsating main street, cascading fourteen pastel-painted blocks down to the bay. With an evocative new rum museum in the bay-side factory once run by the Bacardi family, a name synonymous with the city's history, and a clutch of sights commemorating key events of the Cuban Revolution from which the Bacardis fled, Santiago is an intoxicating blend of old and new.

Street life around Parque Céspedes

Tikal rising from the jungle

TIKAL

Towering above the rainforest, Tikal in Guatemala is possibly the most magnificent of all Maya sites. The ruins are dominated by five enormous temples, steep-sided limestone pyramids that rise to more than 60m above the forest floor. Around them are thousands of other structures, many semi-strangled by giant roots and still hidden beneath mounds of earth.

The site is surrounded by the Parque Nacional Tikal, a protected area of some 576 square kilometres on the edge of the much larger Reserva de la Biósfera Maya. The sheer scale of the place is overwhelming, and its atmosphere spellbinding. Dawn and dusk are the best times to see wildlife, when the forest canopy bursts into a frenzy of sound and activity. The air fills with the screech of toucans and the roar of howler monkeys, while flocks of parakeets wheel around the temples, and bats launch themselves into the night.

Tikal archeological site

Howler monkey, Parque Nacional Tikal

Toucan

OCEANIA

FIJI

Sun-drenched beaches, turquoise lagoons, swaying palm trees – Fiji supplies all the classic images of paradise. No wonder, then, that every year thousands of travellers come to this South Pacific archipelago for the ultimate island escape. But it's not all coral reefs and cocktails: the islands boast dramatic waterfalls, lush rainforests echoing with birdsong, and remote villages where you'll find a traditional way of life continues.

While many people spend their whole time in Fiji sunbathing and sipping cocktails from coconuts, there are plenty of activities on offer, too. Within a ten-minute boat ride of most resorts you can find yourself snorkelling over colourful reefs, sometimes amid dolphins and manta rays, or scuba diving at pristine drop-offs covered in soft corals and sea fans. In addition, at the exposed edges of the reefs are some of the world's finest and most consistent surfing breaks. Further inland is a world of stunning mountains, rainforests and remote villages, where you'll find big-hearted and hospitable Fijians living a lifestyle similar to their tribal ancestors.

Snorkelling off Fiji

Summer hike

Walking between ice sheets

Flying over the glaciated landscape

Mountain hut, Franz Josef Glacier

FRANZ JOSEF GLACIER AND FOX GLACIER

The rugged and pristine landscape of New Zealand's South Island is the stuff of legend. Here on the west coast and just 20km apart, Franz Josef Glacier and Fox Glacier plunge from the Southern Alps almost to the sea – well below the snow line – and you can hear the grinding and cracking of compacted ice as it moves. Legend tells of the beautiful Hine Hukatere who so loved the mountains that she encouraged her lover, Tawe, to climb alongside her. He fell to his death and Hine Hukatere cried so copiously that her tears formed the glaciers, with Franz Josef known to Maori as Ka Roimata o Hine Hukatere – "The Tears of the Avalanche Girl".

Treks to Fox and Franz Josef Glacier take in the lower alpine valley to viewing areas 500m from the terminal face. But to experience the cold blue landscape up close, take a helicopter tour to the top of either glacier and explore deep crevasses, tunnels and ice caves.

Traversing Fox Glacier

Heart of Voh

New Caledonia's capital, Nouméa

Amédée Islet and lighthouse

Isle of Pines

Soursop for sale

NEW CALEDONIA

Locals gather in traditional French markets selling morning-baked baguettes, warm pastries, colourful vegetables and fresh fish in the towns of New Caledonia – a small slice of France in the Pacific Ocean. Palm-fringed beaches lie just beyond, where turquoise waters shelter a healthy abundance of bright corals and marine life. Take in the weird and wonderful creatures who call this home with snorkel and flippers or venture into the deep with full diving gear.

New Caledonia offers ecological oddities including the Isle of Pines, an island covered in columnar pines all the way to its sandy shores, and the Heart of Voh. Seen from above, it really does look like a heart – and it's all natural, created by a clearing in the dense mangroves.

NINGALOO REEF

Bronzed deserts, turquoise shores, rainbow reefs and a posse of creatures big and small, the Ningaloo Coast heralds an alien landscape that gives the Great Barrier Reef a run for its money. As a fringing coral reef, you can swim to the warm and welcoming waters of Ningaloo Reef directly from the beach.

As well as playing host to a whopping five hundred species of fish, three hundred types of coral, dugongs, manta rays, humpback whales and dolphins, this is the best place in Australia – and perhaps the most ethical in the world – to swim with whale sharks. These gentle, intricately patterned giants (the size of a car) frequent the area from March to July – witnessing one emerging through the depths is a heart-racing and humbling experience that can't be matched. Opt to soar above the water in a helicopter or microlight and you'll be rewarded – and mesmerized – by the kaleidoscopic colours and textures of the seascape below and the weird and wonderful life that inhabits it.

Coral Bay, Western Australia

Snorkelling on the reef

Whale shark

On the beach in Cape Range National Park

The World Bar & Restaurant, Queenstown

Jetboating on the Shotover River

View over Queenstown and Lake Wakatipu

The Remarkables

QUEENSTOWN

Queenstown is the adventure capital of New Zealand, superbly set by the deep-blue Lake Wakatipu and hemmed in by craggy mountains. The thin fresh air that descends over the town is filled with the scent of pine and lingering smoke from wood fires during the winter months, when sports enthusiasts from around the globe come to ski and snowboard on the Remarkables. Queenstown has a distinctly European flavour, with its snowy peaks and the still waters of Lake Wakitipu at its centre. Locals and visitors alike gather in cosy restaurants, spilling out onto the pedestrianized streets to trade stories of fun-filled days over a cold beer or a hot chocolate.

This South Island hub hosts all manner of other adventure activities. The most prominent of these is bungee jumping, but rafting, skydiving, paragliding and jetboating are also popular. Best leave these for the summer months, however, when the temperatures have risen and the air has lost its bite.

Wild horses cooling off, Ua Huka Island

Black-tip reef sharks at the Blue Lagoon, Rangiroa

Mo'orea Island

Harpoon fishing

TUAMOTU AND MARQUESAS ISLANDS

We've all heard of Tahiti and Bora Bora, with their bleach-white sands and azure seas, frequented by sun-baked celebs and love-struck honeymooners. Indeed, most visitors to French Polynesia – a collection of 118 islands and atolls in the South Pacific - will opt for one of the Society islands, but a trip to one of the less-visited archipelagos can be even more rewarding.

The Tuamotu islands are seriously off-the-grid; you won't find any shopping or nightlife options here, or even consistent wi-fi. The small coral atoll of Tikehau is particularly enchanting, with pink-sand beaches that slide into crystalline tropical waters. Fishing is still the primary money-maker here, and parts of the atoll are still virtually uninhabited. Nearby Rangiroa – one of the largest atolls in the world – is a diver's dream, with a vast lagoon the size of Tahiti, as well as dolphins, manta rays, barracudas and sharks.

Even more secluded, the Marquesas islands are among the most remote island groups on earth, a three-hour flight from the Society islands and thousands of kilometres from the nearest continent. These raw and rugged islands are breathtakingly beautiful, with white-and black-sand beaches, looming cliffs swathed in green, and wild horses, boars and goats wandering free.

Beach on Tikehau

ULURU

If you're wondering whether all the hype is worth it, the answer is, emphatically, yes. Rising out of the parched red centre of Australia, Uluru (Ayres Rock) is the dramatic touchstone of this ancient continent. The Rock, its textures, colours and not least its elemental presence, is a sacred site to its Aboriginal custodians and without question one of the world's natural wonders.

Uluru means "meeting place", and many Aboriginal dreaming tracks or songlines intersect here. Spirituality is often grounded in more practical draws, and Uluru, with its permanent water hole, abundant animal life, shelter and firewood, has been saving lives for millennia. The rock is sacred to the local Anangu people, who resumed ownership of the lands inside the national park in 1985, in a historic handover ceremony.

Uluru

INDEX

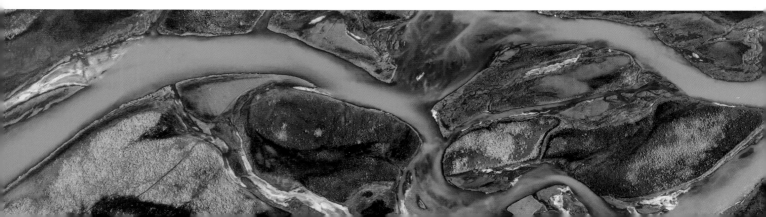

CONTRIBUTORS

Jacqui Agate

Aga Bylica

Susie Boulton

Chris Bradley

Philip Briggs

Jess Cropper

Donna Dailey

Steph Dyson

Helen Fanthorpe

Dinah Gardner

Lottie Gross

Rebecca Hallett

Tim Hannigan

Nick Inman

Anthon Jackson

Joe Legate

Jeroen van Marle

Sîan Marsh

Shafik Meghji

Stephanie Mitchell

Rachel Mills

Chris Moss

Matt Norman

Joanne Owen

Alan Palmer

Kirsten Powley

Joanna Reeves

Zara Sekhavati

Daniel Stables

Paul Stafford

Aimee White

Lizzie Williams

PHOTO CREDITS

(Key: T-top; C-centre; B-bottom; L-left; R-right)